E2

The Glass Circle 4

AF574672

Edited by
R. J. Charleston
Wendy Evans and
Ada Polak

Gresham Books

© The Glass Circle
First published 1982.

ISBN 0 946095 02 7

The Glass Circle

President:
R. J. Charleston

Honorary Vice-Presidents:
Dr. Donald B. Harden, FSA
Paul Perrot
G. H. Tait

Committee:
Miss W. Evans
Dr. H. J. Kersley
Mrs. B. Morris
C. Truman
E. T. Udall
Dr. D. C. Watts
Cyril Weeden

Honorary Secretary:
Mrs. C. G. Benson

Honorary Treasurer:
P. H. Whatmoor, ACA,
43, Lancaster Road, London, W11 1QJ.

Copies of *The Glass Circle 4* may be obtained from the publisher at a cost of £9.50 (postage extra: weight packed 15 oz/400 grams). For *The Glass Circle 1-3*, see inside back cover.

Published by Gresham Books and printed by Unwin Brothers Limited, Old Woking, Surrey, GU22 9LH.

Contents

Illustrations

Some English Glass-Engravers: late 18th-early 19th century

by R. J. CHARLESTON

A Paper read to the Circle on 20 February, 1975.

It has often been rubbed into us, in the literature of glass, that English engraving was never up to much, and that in any case the first engravers in this country were of German or Bohemian origin (which is no doubt true). Perhaps for this reason —a generally underdog sort of attitude to the subject—little really seems to have been done to identify the wheel-engraved work of the 18th and early 19th century, an omission encouraged also by the circumstance that English engraving of this period seems on the whole to be in fact somewhat stereotyped and unenterprising. Perhaps when Dr. Seddon gives us his paper in May, we shall begin to look at this question with new eyes.[1]

My task is in some ways simpler, since I propose to stick to engravers whose names are known and sometimes also whose works are known through signatures. I should also make it clear that I shall be dealing only with wheel-engravers, and not with practitioners of the diamond-point.

Although I do not propose to give a long historical retrospect, it may perhaps be convenient at the outset to clear up two points, the first technical, the second historical. First, technique. Wheel-engraving on glass, as its name implies, is executed by means of a series of (usually copper) wheels of varying diameter and thickness, on to the edge of which an abrasive (usually, at the period we are considering, emery-powder) is fed in an oily medium. The depth of the cutting governs the apparent relief of the modelling of the subject engraved. These cuts with the harder metal wheels can subsequently be polished with wheels of progressively softer material (pewter, lead, wood, cork, etc.) using abrasives of a diminishing harshness (tripoli, putty-powder, etc.). Second, history. Opinions have differed as to just when wheel-engraving was introduced into this country, and in the absence of any decisive evidence, it is probably not very profitable to speculate upon the point. Suffice it to say that on 30 August, 1735, the following advertisement appeared in the *Daily Journal:* 'The Glass Sellers Arms. Where are to be had the best Double Flint Glass, Diamond-Cut and Plain, with several curiosities engraved on Glass . . .'[2] The wording of this last phrase is a pretty good indication that the items referred to were in the van of fashion. This advertisement was inserted by one Benjamin Payne, who had already referred, in an earlier advertisement dated 12 June to 'the Arms of all the Royal Family finely engraved on glasses'.[3] It might be objected that the wording of these advertisements is no absolute guarantee that this work was executed in Benjamin Payne's workshop, or even in this country—let alone that Payne himself was a glass-engraver; but there seems a strong possibility that he was. Curiously enough, the year 1735 also brings us a notice of a man who most certainly was a glass-engraver—one Joseph Martin, then referred to significantly as the only glass-engraver in Ireland. His advertisement ran: 'Whereas several gentlemen and ladies whose curiosity led them to have their arms, crests, words, letters or figures carved on their glass ware, and as several have had cause to complain of the extravagant prices, these are therefore to advertise the public that Joseph Martin living in Fleet Street, Dublin, opposite the Golden Ball, is the only person that was employed by the managers of the glass house in Fleet Street in carving the said wares, and that there is no other person in the kingdom that does profess to do the like work. He therefore having broken off with the said gentlemen does propose to deal more candidly with those as are pleased to employ him by working at such moderate rates as none hereafter may have reason to complain.'[4] A John Martin, a substantial London glass-grinder, is mentioned in the *British Mercury* for 24 February, 1714, and crops up again in Probate Court of Canterbury *Inventories* for 14 September, 1726, shown as a glass-grinder of St. Martins in the Fields.[5] Joseph Martin is very likely to have been related to this man, and to have come from London, which was unquestionably the seminal centre for developments in the glass-industry at this period.

Beginning in 1742 Jerome Johnson, of the Entire Glass Shop, at the corner of St. Martin's Lane, issued a long series of advertisements listing 'flowered glasses', and implying that he was the maker of the objects he listed.[6] That Johnson did in fact execute, or have executed, in his workshop the glasses that he lists seems evident from two later advertisements which Francis Buckley found but was not able to include in his *History of Old English Glass*. The first occurred in the *London Evening Post* for a number of issues in February and March of 1751: 'For Glass-engraving or flowering, cutting, scalloping and finest polishing upon Glass in general. At the Intire Glass Shop, over against the New Exchange in the Strand . . .' The second fell some five years later, in November, 1756: 'Jerom Johnson, at the entire Glass Shop . . . is determined to sell off all, and retire into the Country, by Lady-Day next. The whole Stock in Trade consists of various Cut-Glasses and others; . . . Also working tools, Lapidary Benches, Scalloper's Mills, Glass Flowerers and Engraving Tools (too Tedious to mention). All to be sold cheap.'[7] Despite all these protestations, he was still in business in 1760. One can only guess whether Johnson himself had ever been an executant engraver, but if he had, it seems likely that he must long since have relinquished that activity in favour of organising an obviously large-scale workshop. As was set forth in *A General Description of all Trades* (published in London in 1747): 'Glass-Sellers. These are a set of Shop-keepers, and some of them very large Dealers, whose only Business is to sell all sorts of White Flint Glass, who may very properly come under this Title; though here and there one are Masters also of the Art of *Scolloping glass*, which is now greatly in vogue'. The firm of Maydwell and Windle's, at the King's Arms in the Strand, which seems never to have advertised, but which almost certainly was in a big way of business, as may be seen from their tradecard[8], seems to reflect the same sort of situation. At the bottom of their trade-card is added the sentence 'Engraving on Glasses of every kind in the Newest Taste at ye most Reasonable Rates'. This, taken in conjunction with the scenes of cutting illustrated at the bottom of their card, very strongly suggests that the work was done on the premises. In the same way, but at a later date, W. G. Cave announced himself on his trade-card as 'Glass Cutter, Manufacturer of Cut Glass in all its Branches . . . 157 Fenchurch Street, near Lime Street, London. Glass Engraver, Chemical Stopperer . . . (fig. 1). As with Maydwell and Windle, the card shows cutters (both overhand and underhand) at work, and we may reasonably surmise that the engraving too was done on the premises. But in neither case do we know who the engraver was.

What happened in London was echoed, after a due lapse of time, in the provinces. In 1749, for instance, Richard Matthews, whom those of you who were present will remember from Miss Sheenah Smith's paper on the Norwich glass-sellers, advertised on the 29th July that at his new address he continued to 'sell all sorts of ground, Flowered and wormed Glasses at the lowest Price, according to their work . . .'[9] Matthews almost certainly got his glasses ready-made from London, but another retailer of London glasses in a provincial centre, Phillip Elliott, of Clare Street, Bristol, when in December, 1785, he advertised 'an elegant assortment of cut and plain glass', added 'N. B. Glass cut and engraved to any pattern, as he keeps a glass cutter and engraver'.[10] We do not know who this man was, but the *Universal British Directory* of 1790 records a James Padmore, 'Glass-engraver, of 11 Somerset Square, Bristol', and in the same *Directory* John Percival, described as a 'Glassman' lived at the same address (12, Union Street) as Messrs. Parr and Wright 'engravers', who might of course have been ordinary copper-plate engravers, but whose sharing the same address with a glassman suggests that they may in fact have been glass-engravers. No work attributable to any of these men is recorded, so far as I know. W. Matthews, in his *New History, Survey and Description of the City . . . of Bristol* . . ., published in 1794, lists, apart from the men already recorded:

> William Clark Glass-cutter and Engraver, Temple Street.
> Jacob Samuel, Glass engraver, Temple Street.
> Joseph Smith, Glass engraver, Cathay.

One has the impression that by this date—the 80s and 90s of the 18th century—the glass-engraver was beginning to emerge as an artistic personality in his own right, whereas in the middle and third quarter of the century he was just one craftsman among others in a workshop. Bernard Hughes in his *English, Scottish and Irish Table Glass* quotes an advertisement from the *Weekly Mercury* in July, 1771 for a 'glasscutter and flowerer', who would no doubt have carried his skill into the atelier of his new master.[11] Such a man would have submerged his personality in anonymity, whereas when we approach the end of the 18th century, we begin to get glasses signed by the artists who executed them.

The first of our identifiable signing engravers is a man named John Unsworth. Wigan Corporation is the appropriate owner of a tumbler (which was shown in the 1968 Exhibition of English Glass held in the Victoria and Albert Museum, No. 256) cut round the base with flutes and inscribed: 'PROSPERATION (sic) TO THE CORPORATION', and on the reverse: 'A GIFT TO THE WORTHY CORPORATION OF WIGAN FROM JOHN UNSWORTH, CUT AND ENGRAV'D GLASS MANUFACTURER TO HIS MAJESTY AND HIS ROYAL HIGHNESS THE PRINCE OF WALES, MANCHESTER'. (fig. 2). It stands some $4\frac{1}{2}$ inches high. We know that John Unsworth was elected a Burgess of Wigan on 4 October, 1800, so this is no doubt the date to be put on this glass, which, after being missing from the Corporation's collection of plate and other treasures, was restored to it by purchase in 1939. As luck would have it, I came across Unsworth's trade-card in the Banks Collection in the British Museum (fig. 3). Somebody has written in ink at top and bottom the date 1792, which seems reasonable enough, although no warrant is given for it.

Nothing else seems to be known about this man. It is worth recalling, however, that on 22 December, 1795, *The Manchester Mercury* carried an advertisement by Atherton and Whalley, 'Cut and Engraved Glass Manufacturers . . . have opened a shop at 3 Market Street-lane, and laid in a large and elegant assortment of ornamental and plain goods. N.B. Glasses of all sorts cut to any pattern.'[12] Clearly therefore cutting was done on the premises, and the title 'Cut and Engraved Glass Manufacturers' at this date seems to imply that the firm did its own work, despite the flavour of shop-keeping conveyed by the wording of the advertisement. It would be worth bearing in mind that Unsworth might have worked for this firm as well as on his own account. The Athertons were a Liverpool glass-making family.[13]

In Liverpool itself we find one Thomas Billinge, described as 'glass-flowerer', recorded in *Directories* between 1767 and 1800.[14] *Gore's Directory* for 1773 records one Thomas Skidmore at Hanover Street; and this man is shown in 1803 as 'glass engraver',[15] so it may reasonably be assumed that for thirty years he followed the calling of glass-engraver, without leaving a single identifiable glass behind him. *Gore's General Advertiser* for 11 September, 1800, carries an advertisement: 'James Holt, Glass Cutter and Engraver No. 51 Lord St., Respectfully informs the Nobility Gentry and public in general, in the town and neighbourhood of Liverpool, he has opened the above shop, where he purposes selling all sorts of *Plain, Cut,* and *Engraved Glass,* on the lowest terms. N.B. *Arms, Crests,* and *Cyphers* are ably engraved on the shortest notice. Orders for exportation thankfully received and duly executed.' A firm by the name of Thomas Holt & Co., Glass Manufactory, of Hanover Street, flourished between 1781 and 1790, but there is no evidence to suggest whether these two concerns were in any way connected.[16]

A third Liverpool engraver was John Pattison, who is shown in *Gore's Directory* of 1810 as being established at 1, Tristram Court.[17]

From the north-west we may now perhaps turn our eyes towards the north-east, where a few glasses as well as a few names may be found.

Francis Buckley in *A History of Old English Glass*[18] quotes Boyle's *Vestiges of Old Newcastle* (1890) in recording: 'Mr. Charles W. Henzell of Tynemouth possesses a magnificent glass bowl, questionless of Tyneside manufacture, on which these (the Henzell) arms are engraved with the name and date, 'John Henzell, 1756''. The bowl itself seems to have disappeared, but a decanter with three-ringed neck, engraved with a bird and the rose, thistle and shamrock symbolic of the Union of the three Kingdoms with Ireland (after 1801), bears also the name 'Tyzack' engraved on it. This name, and the fact that the decanter is in the Laing Art Gallery at Newcastle, strongly suggest that it was made and engraved on Tyneside. The same is true of a probably somewhat earlier tankard (fig. 4), acquired for the Victoria and Albert Museum in 1958 together with a silver medallion inscribed: 'Samuel the Second Borne Sonn of John and Sarah Tizacke Was borne att the Glass House New Castle ye 27 of September Anno Domini 1677.' The tankard itself is engraved with hops and barley and the inscription: 'G. Tyzack, Glass Maker'. Unfortunately, it has not so far been possible to identify this member of the Tyzack family, but the association of the tankard with the silver medallion makes it most likely that it too was produced and engraved on Tyneside. These two glasses are alas! anonymous, but the names of some contemporary Newcastle engravers are known. Francis Buckley records from the *Newcastle Directories:*[19]

Thomas Alexander	1778-95
Isaac Levy	1778
Robert Hudson	1787
E. Jackson	1795

Thomas Alexander is first mentioned in J.R. Boyle, *The First Newcastle Directory, 1778* (1889) under the heading 'Glass Grinders and Flowerers', as being 'near Close Gate', the area in which most of the flint glasshouses found themselves. In W. Whitehead's *Account of Newcastle upon Tyne,* published in 1787, he is shown as 'glass-cutter and engraver, west-end of the Close', so he really was an engraver. In the same author's *Newcastle and Gateshead Directory for 1790* he is shown simply as 'glass-engraver, &c., without Close Gate'; and in Hilton's 1795 *Directory* as 'glass-engraver, without Close Gate'. He therefore had a career of more than twenty years as an engraver in Newcastle, but nothing can be attributed to him. The Isaac Levi of the 1778 *Directory,* however, does not appear again in the later *Directories,* and was perhaps a rolling stone like his namesake Henry Levy, recorded in the *London Gazette* for 15 September, 1772, as 'Fugitive debtor . . . Henry Levy, formerly of Stourbridge, late of Shoemaker Row, London, glass-flowerer'.[20] A Mordecai Levi 'Glass Engraver and China Mender', is recorded at the China Jar, near Exeter Change, the Strand, in 1765,[21] so glass-engraving seems to have run in this family. We know nothing of the work of any of these Levys.

With Robert Hudson, the third on Buckley's list, we get on to firmer ground. He is mentioned in Whitehead's *Account of Newcastle* . . . in 1787 as 'glass cutter and engraver, Closegate'; and in the 1795 *Newcastle and Gateshead Directory* as 'glass cutter, Close'. He was still going strong in 1803, for in May of that year he rendered an account to the Assembly Rooms for 'Repairing one Jerrendole', the bill having a printed head 'Bought of Robert Hudson Glass-cutter and Engraver', thus confirming that he had in fact been an engraver throughout the period.[22] W. A. Thorpe, in 'Some Types of Newcastle Glass', (*Antiques*, June, 1933, p. 208), writes: 'The name of R. Hudson (Robert Hudson) occurs in Newcastle Directories for 1787 as a cutter and engraver of glass. There is reason to believe that Thomas Hudson, who was probably his son, occupied a glasshouse on a site near the Close, later in the hands of Sowerby's, and that he was a manufacturer as well as an engraver of glass. A record exists of a christening glass dated 1787 which was made and engraved by Thomas Hudson. Another glass engraved by him carried a view of St. Andrew's Church, Newcastle, with his own name and that of his wife Margaret. Made to commemorate his second marriage, it is dated 1808 . . . ' Unfortunately, it has not been possible to trace either of these glasses, and one may feel a little sceptical of a glass engraved by Thomas Hudson as early as 1787, when his father was still living in 1803, and he himself was not mentioned in the 1787 *Directory*. Thomas Hudson was still active in 1836, when he is recorded as 'glass-cutter' in the *Newcastle Directory*, occupying premises in Nun's Lane and at 13 Woodbine-Terrace, Gateshead. He does not appear in *Pigot's Directory* of 1837, however, so he may have died or given up work in the meantime; although absence from a Directory is by no means decisive evidence. For Thomas Hudson, however, it is at last possible to produce a glass—a rummer engraved with Neptune driving his car, signed 'T. Hudson eng. Newcastle, No. 9'—probably familiar to many either from Mr. Thorpe's article, or from Mr. Wakefield's *19th Century British Glass*.[23] The former draws analogies with the glasses engraved to commemorate Nelson's death in 1805; the latter prefers a date about 1840. The glass was shown in the 1968 Exhibition (*Catalogue* No. 265).

Of the E. Jackson recorded in the 1795 *Newcastle and Gateshead Directory* as 'glass-cutter and engraver, Quayside' nothing more seems to be known. There was, however, a Thomas Jackson in the glass business, a 'Turner and Glass-cutter' in Mutton Lane, Clerkenwell, in 1785[24]: and it is no doubt to this concern that Mr. Blakeway, of 'Blakeway and Hodsdon, Cut and Plain Glass Manufactory . . . No. 71, Strand . . . ' referred when he called himself 'Blakeway from Jacksons Manufactory, Clerkenwell'.[25] Glass-cutting may have run in the Jackson family.

A somewhat later Newcastle engraver was John Williams, who is referred to in the 1824 *Directory* as 'Glass engraver, Middle Street'. In the 1838 and 1839 *Directories* he is described as 'Glass engraver and dealer in glass, 18 Pilgrim Street', and in 1847 as 'John Williams, Engraver, 18 Pilgrim Street'. From his hand we have at least one piece, a jug in the Nelson Museum, Monmouth (fig. 5), shown in the 1968 Exhibition as No. 264. It is decorated with vertical flutes round the base, and is engraved with figures of 'Fame', 'Britannia', etc., symbolizing Lord Nelson's victories at sea. It is signed on the base in diamond-point 'John Williams Engraver, Newcastle' (fig. 6). The shape of the jug would suggest that it was made perhaps towards the beginning of his recorded career rather than at the end of it, although the Nelson cult was going strong about the middle of the 19th century.

Glasses which enjoyed a singular popularity on Tyneside and probably also elsewhere, were the rummers engraved with a view of the Sunderland Bridge, opened in 1796, but commemorated thereafter for fifty years or more. So far as I know, none of these is actually signed, but it seems likely that some at least of them were engraved by members of the Haddock family at Sunderland — Thomas, who was born in 1797 and died in 1866, and Robert, who is apparently recorded in the Sunderland *Directory* for 1834, and went on until about 1860.[26] It was no doubt a collateral who is mentioned in the *Cork Evening Post* of 17 January, 1793—one Marsden Haddock, of Cork, who 'supplies Cork and Waterford glass, does the cutting himself, and also employes (sic) a cutter from England.'[27]

Before moving south from Tyneside, I should refer to one engraver whose name is recorded and who may have worked in that region. In the Art Treasures Exhibition held in 1932 Messrs. Cecil Davis showed a table-service from Lambton Castle decorated with heavy cutting and engraved with the arms of the Earl of Durham. One fingerbowl from this service was stated to bear the signature 'Greener sculp.'[28] A Robert Greener is recorded as an engraver at Sunderland in the second quarter of the 19th century.[29] It is worth bearing in mind that in the Newcastle Procession of Glassmakers in 1823, one of the items carried by the glassmen of the Wear (from Messrs. White and Young) was 'A Prince of Wales' decanter, with four wines, and engraved with the arms of J. G. Lambton, esq.'[30] Lambton was the family name of the Earls of Durham.

One last glass should be mentioned in this context—a rummer once in the possession of Mr. Howard Phillips, engraved with a view of Newcastle Bridge, and signed 'R. YOUNG'. I have not been able to find any trace of this man, but the subject of the glass suggests Tyneside and a date in or slightly after 1835.

Let us now turn south, merely noticing as we go that *Etherington's York Chronicle* for 22 July, 1774, carries an advertisement: 'Thomas Surr, shopman to the late Mr. Marfitt, Glass Seller, has purchased his late master's stock in trade, consisting of a large and elegant assortment of Cut, Flowered and Plain Glass, and purposes carrying on the business in all its branches in the same shop. The same hands are engaged for cutting and engraving.' From March 1775 until July, 1778, Surr advertised in the same journal 'the best manufactured cut engraved and plain glass of the newest and most fashionable patterns. Gentlemen may have glass cut or engraved to any pattern as well as in London, upon very short notice',[31] an indication that the work was still being done on the premises.

One of the first indications of engraving at Stourbridge comes to us, perhaps significantly, from the north. The *Newcastle Chronicle* for 30 December, 1769, records: 'Samuel Richards, apprentice to Pidcock, Ensell and Bradley, to the glass-engraving business, near Stourbridge, absconded his masters' service'. I have already mentioned Henry Levy, the fugitive debtor formerly of Stourbridge, who was a 'glass-flowerer', and a curiously parallel case is that of Samuel Benedict in 1767, an 'engraver of glass' who, being bankrupt, went off to London. He is presumably the same S. Benedict recorded in the *Manchester Mercury* for 1 November, 1785, as having 'arrived from London at Manchester with a large quantity of all kinds of cut glass in the present fashion . . . '[32] For every glass-engraver who ran away, there were presumably several who stayed put. One of these was Thomas Dudley, recorded as an engraver in Dudley in the 1790 *Directory*.[33] As far as I know, no single 18th century wheel-engraved glass can confidently be attributed to the Stourbridge district. When we come to the 19th century, however, the picture brightens. Shortly before our preparations began for the 1968 Exhibition, a large rummer was brought to the Museum by a Mr. A. R. Fenn-Wiggin. It was engraved with a coach and four, inscribed on the door: 'London and Aylesbury', and on the reverse with the initials J. J. W. within a wreath. It was signed 'W. Herbert Eng. Dudley'. Although not dated, its date was suggested by the fact that the coach-owner's name ('Hearm' for 'Joseph Hearn') was inscribed on the coach-door, and this man is recorded as running waggons and coaches between London and Aylesbury in 1830 and 1837. The driver of the coach was a certain James Wyatt, whose initials are presumably those on the bowl.[34] William Herbert had already been brought into the literature by Mr. Wakefield in his *19th Century British Glass*,[35] as working for the Dudley firm of Thomas Hawkes, a connection which was confirmed by the form of the signature on this glass. In 1835 the firm was stated to have produced an important presentation 'plateau' both engraved and etched by William Herbert. No trace of this presumably ambitious piece apparently survives. Herbert's *oeuvre* has, however, recently been greatly extended by a number of pieces which came to light in an auction in the West Country and found their way to London. A claret-jug at present on loan to the Victoria and Albert Museum is both embellished with cutting of high quality, and engraved with another coaching-scene, the coach this time being inscribed 'The Road', 'The Wonder, Birmingham-Stourbridge-London' and the signature 'W. Herbert' '1883' (fig. 7). Two virtually identical claret-jugs remain in private hands, the first also with a coaching-scene, signed 'W. Herbert' and dated 1828. In case it should be thought that Herbert could engrave nothing but coaches, the second of these decanters is decorated with a hunting-scene, inscribed 'The Field' in exactly the same way as the jug with 'The Road', although it is not signed.

In nearby Birmingham, the firm of T. Illidge and Son advertised in *Wrightson's Triennial Directory of Birmingham* (1818) that they had set up in business in Cherry Street, coming from West Smithfield, London. Illidge referred to himself primarily as 'Glass Engraver', and his advertisement makes clear that the work was done on the premises (fig. 8).

Illidge came from London, and in the capital there must have been great numbers of glass-engravers at work, their identity concealed beneath the names of the larger *entrepreneurs* for whom, or in whose workshops, they worked. We have already noted the cases of Benjamin Payne, Jerome Johnson, Maydwell and Windle, Mordecai Levy and S. Benedict. In 1773 a Philadelphia newspaper recorded 'Lazarus Isaac, Glass Cutter and Engraver on Glass . . . being just arrived from London', who went to work for Stiegel only a month after arriving in Philadelphia.[36] Later on in London there were W. G. Cave and T. Illidge, both already referred to. The following are recorded in the *Universal Directory* of 1790:

George Armstead, glass-engraver and cutter, New Street Square.
James Byrne, glass-engraver, 79 Little Britain.
Thomas Frankland, glass-cutter and engraver, 59 Redcross Street, Cripplegate.

No glasses can be connected with these three craftsmen.

A certain Samuel Collings is listed in this *Directory* as 'Lapidary and glass-cutter', of Earl Street, Seven Dials, and this combination of crafts strongly suggests that he may have been a glass-engraver too. In the Victoria and Albert Museum is a rummer with lemon-squeezer foot, engraved with a formal border and the initials EM; below the initials is the diamond-point signature 'Collins Engraver'. This signature has always hitherto been associated with the name of William Collins, a well-known glass-maker at 227 The Strand, at one time a member of the partnership of Perry and Collins at that address. This man is recorded as a stained glass artist, a likelihood borne out by his trade-card in the Banks Collection in the British Museum, running: 'Gallery of Stain'd and Painted Glass. Wm. Collins Glass Manufacturer to Her Majesty and the Royal Family . . . Extensive variety of Lustres and Grecian Lamps and Cut Glass of every description . . .' This is dated in ink '1815'. There is nothing in all this to make one suppose that this illustrious *entrepreneur* would engrave with his own hands a simple glass and sign it as 'engraver'. Perhaps the artist was indeed Samuel Collings, the mistake in a name in the 1790 *Directory* being a commonplace occurrence for that compilation.

The second identifiable London engraver whom I have been able to trace was brought to my notice by a jug then in the possession of Cecil Davis (fig. 9). It bore on the front the arms of the City of London, and was accompanied by a hand-written card signed by a certain John Pye, to the effect that the jug had been engraved by his ancestor, another John Pye, for the Lord Mayor's Banquet of Alderman Bull, who was inducted into the Mayoralty in 1773. This date did not seem to agree with the probable date of the jug on stylistic grounds. I was finally able through the Free Masons' Hall to get in touch with living members of the Pye family. The Family Bible, in the possession of Miss E. D. Pye, of Ipswich, contains the following entry: 'John Pye, Glass Engraver, London born March 20th 1822 as son of John Pye, Glass Engraver, Freeman of (the) City of London . . .', and a number of glasses remain in the hands of this lady.[37] Unfortunately, as their style proclaims, these must have been the work of John Pye, junior. Fortunately, Robson's *Directory* of London, published in 1833, contains the first traced entry for a John Pye, glass engraver, he being then resident at 11 Redlion Court, Fleet Street.[38] An earlier reference, however, is contained in a hand-written *Memoir* of a certain George Perry, who was partner in the famous London firm of Perry and Parker, under the date 1819: 'Went with Richard (Perry) and Pye to Snaresbrook Augt 29th'.[39] It seems evident that at this date the elder John Pye was employed by this firm. The business was mainly concerned with the manufacture of glass chandeliers and lighting-fittings; and, like T. Illidge, Pye no doubt engraved the borders on the candle-shades which normally formed part of the chandeliers made at this period. When the firm of Perry and Parker supplied chandeliers to Goldsmith's Hall in 1835, the estimates included a memorandum: 'Engraving the Glass Shades with Vine Border 2s. 9d. each shade extra'.[40] So far, however, only one other glass by John Pye has been traced — a mirror engraved with the representation of a sailing ship, signed 'J. Pye', in the possession of our member, Dr. Richard Emanuel.

A large rummer in the possession of a former Circle member, Lady Black, is engraved with an emblem of the Glass Makers' Friendly Society, and is signed 'Eng. by A. Conne'.[41] This man is probably to be identified with the Augustin Conne who showed engraved glass in the Great Exhibition of 1851.[42] He is first mentioned in a Directory for 1852, his name continuing until 1859. He was presumably the son of Nicholas Conne, glass engraver, first mentioned in *Pigot's Directory* for 1823-4 as 'Nichs. Come' (*sic*) and continuing until 1854, after which his name disappears. In 1856 'Conne & Goodwin', 'designers in glass & manufacturers, engravers & cutters to the trade' are mentioned at the same address as Nicholas Conne's and continued there until 1868. After 1859 the Conne of this partnership was probably Mrs. Emily Conne, also described as 'engraver on glass' and first mentioned in 1860. She was presumably Augustin's widow.[43]

In 1784 (10 July) the *Norwich Mercury* carried an advertisement: 'Yarmouth. Glass, China and Earthenwares. William Absolon, Junior (who last Year took the Stock in Trade of Mrs. E. Clabon, on her retiring from Business) . . . [He] has lately laid in a fresh assortment from the best Manufactories . . . and a Number of other Articles which he is enabled to sell on the cheapest Terms, at his Shop, the lower end of the Market Row . . .' In May, 1785, he had a trade-card engraved, by which time he was established at 4, Market Row: this advertised among other things: 'a great Variety of cut and plain GLASS and EARTHEN-WARES of all Kinds, from the best Manufactories in the Kingdom.' In fact, Absolon derived his stocks of both ceramics and glass from a number of sources, of which the most important was almost certainly London. His painted and gilt glasses are frequently identifiable by the fact that they are signed. With engraved glasses the situation is obviously more difficult, since they are not signed. Absolon's later trade-card, showing him as dealing from 25, Market Row, adds: 'Where he has a Manufactory for Enamelling & Gilding his Goods, with Coats of Arms . . . (etc.) N.B. Glass Cut or Engraved to pattern on Short Notice.' From this it has been concluded that the engraving was done on the premises, but the wording of the card perhaps rather suggests that there was a distinction between the enamelling and gilding, done on the premises, and the engraving done at short notice. Be that as it may, there are a number of glasses which by their Yarmouth and generally East Anglian subject-matter, and their affinities of shape and style, clearly indicate that they emanated from Absolon's shop. There is no evidence that he himself was an engraver, but we may safely refer to this craftsman as the 'Absolon engraver'.[44]

POSTSCRIPT

Since this paper was compiled, a number of further pieces of information have come to notice. Some of them have already been set out in the foot-notes to this paper (n. 21, Arthur Jacob; n. 26, R. Pyle; n. 29, Thomas Bulmer).

Our member Mrs. Arlene Palmer Schwind has kindly drawn to my attention three further British engravers who migrated to America—John Moss (in Philadelphia, 1796-1800) and Moses Moss (1797); and James Hay (1774-1826) from Scotland, who sojourned at Chelmsford, Mass., 1810-26.

An important reference, culled from the list of Employers in the Register of Apprentices in the Public Record Office, was kindly brought to my notice by Mr. Eric Benton: '1766 Joseph Koonert, Glass Engraver, St. Mary le Strand.' Koonert was evidently a member of the important Thuringian glass-making family of Kühnert. A Joseph Kühnert is recorded as a master glassmaker at Henriettenthal (Sachsen-Saalfeld) in 1834, so the Christian name Joseph may have run in this family.[45] He may well have been practising his craft for many years previous to 1766.

H. Clifford Smith, *Buckingham Palace,* London (1931), p. 137, records that a glass-cutter or -engraver named Wainwright executed the sky-lights in the Guard Chamber of Buckingham Palace, apparently in or before 1831 (information kindly supplied by Mr. John Harris).[46] This simple decoration (fig. 10) appears to be executed by 'intaglio engraving'.

The account-books of the London firm of silver-smiths Parker and Wakelin (in the Victoria and Albert Museum Library) record a long account with the London glass-making enterprise of Blakeway and Hodsdon, whose trade-card (in the British Museum) shows them at No. 71, The Strand, apparently in 1797: the partnership seems to have been dissolved in the following year (*London Gazette,* 15 December, 1798, reference found by F. Buckley). On 1 November, 1798, however, they charged Parker & Wakelin 1/4d. 'By Engraving 4 Liquor Bottles'; so they too must have had an engraver on their staff.

An otherwise undocumented engraver named Coles decorated a small oval plaque shown to the Victoria and Albert Museum some years ago (fig. 11). Its somewhat unskilful decoration probably dates from the years about 1800. It is perhaps worth mentioning that in 1780 James Cole (*sic*) 'Decorator', showed at the Society of Arts a 'Specimen of a new invented, painted and set christalline ornament for Coach Pannels, Tablets, etc.'[47]

As might be expected, evidence has come to light that Jonathan Collet, Thomas Betts's successor at The King's Arms, Charing Cross, employed an engraver on his staff, even if he was not an engraver himself. A bill in the Henry Francis Dupont Winterthur Museum dated 2 July, 1781, and rendered to the Revd. Thomas Moore, includes '2 Burgundy Decanters neatly cut and engraved £2. 2. 0'. This evidence confirms the interpretation of a second bill, in the Victoria and Albert Museum Library. Dated 3 July, 1786, and rendered to 'Mr. Morris, Dover Street' it includes 'Christed (i.e. presumably crested) Champagnes to Patt^{n}: £6 (?)'

The Winterthur Museum also possesses a bill dated 9 May, 1788, rendered to 'Mr. Michie' by 'Standfield & Smith'. On the printed bill-head the '& Smith' have been scratched out by pen. This conforms with the known history of the firm, for *The World* of 6 May, 1788, records that John Smith was leaving the partnership 'Standfield & Smith'. The bill includes the item: '12 Best Wines with Eng^{d} Bord(ers) 7s.'

A renewed perusal of Messrs. Churchill's *History in Glass* (London (1937), p. 38, No. 172) turned up a tumbler engraved with a coat of arms and inscribed: 'Prosperity to the House of Downing.' A further inscription records that 'the glass was made by Mr. John Parrish of Wordsley near Stourbridge, to commemorate the coming-of-age of David Pennant, Esq.: the names of the donors are given and the date 1817'. D. R. Guttery[48] records Wordsley glass-cutters named James and Thomas Parrish, who were bankrupt by 1803. It seems most likely that the glass was engraved in the workshop of John Parrish, whether by himself or an engraver employed by him.

Finally, a John France 'glass engraver' is listed at 1 King Street, Snowhill, in the London *Directory* of 1799.

NOTES

1. This paper was read on 20 February, 1975. Dr. Seddon's paper, entitled 'The Jacobite Glass Engravers' and read on 13 May, 1975, was printed in *The Glass Circle,* No. 3 (1979), pp. 40-78.
2. F. Buckley, *A History of Old English Glass,* London (1925), p. 120, No. 8(b) (Abbreviation: *OEG*).
3. *Ibid.,* No. 8(a) and foot-note.
4. M. S. Dudley Westropp, *Irish Glass,* London (n.d., 1920), p. 49, quoting the *Dublin Evening Post* of February, 1735.
5. P. C. C. Inventories List Probate 3, in P. R. O. 1718-82 (1726, Part II 25/157. 14 September 'John Martin St. Martin's in the Fields. *Glass Grinder'* (reference kindly supplied by Miss Nathalie Rothstein). Martin is mentioned in the *Evening Post* for 12 February, 1713, and insured his goods with the Sun Fire Insurance Office (*British Mercury,* 24 February, 1714). Both these references are from F. Buckley's unpublished list of London glassmen (Guildhall Library).
6. For Johnson, see F. Buckley, *OEG,* pp. 120-1; W. A. Thorpe, *A History of English and Irish Glass,* London (1929), pp. 239, 241, 246-8, 313, 323 (Abbreviation: *History*); *id., English Glass,* London (3rd ed. 1961), pp. 201, 216-20.
7. F. Buckley, 'Great Names in the History of English Glass, VII—Jerom Johnson', *Glass* (September, 1928), pp. 392-3.
8. Illustrated G. Bernard Hughes, *English, Scottish and Irish Table Glass,* London (1956), fig. 28.
9. Sheenah Smith, 'Glass in 18th century Norwich', *The Glass Circle,* 2 (1975), p. 55.
10. Buckley, *OEG,* p. 134, No. 60.
11. Hughes, *op. cit.,* p. 141.
12. Buckley, *OEG,* p. 138, No. 83.
13. James Atherton is recorded there in 1761, William Atherton appears in the Liverpool Freeman's Register in 1735, and William Atherton, junior, is recorded in 1754 and 1761 (P. Entwistle's notes in Liverpool Public Library).
14. Buckley, *OEG,* p. 141.
15. F. Buckley, 'Old Lancashire Glasshouses', *Transactions of the Society of Glass Technology,* 13 (1929), p. 237; the 1803 reference derives from Entwistle's notes (see n. 13).
16. Based on P. Entwistle's notes.
17. Based on P. Entwistle's notes.
18. *Op. cit.,* p. 146, No. 112.
19. *Ibid.,* p. 141.
20. F. Buckley, 'Notes on the Glasshouses of Stourbridge', *Transactions of the Society of Glass Technology,* 11 (1927), p. 121.
21. When he took out a policy with the Sun Insurance Company (Vol. 161, p. 485, No. 221405, kindly communicated by Miss N. Rothstein). See also Zoë Josephs, 'Jewish Glass-makers', *Jewish Historical Society of England, Transactions,* XXV (1977), p. 109, who adds that Mordecai Levy trained up Arthur Jacob as an engraver and Isaac Levy. The latter was no doubt the Newcastle engraver. Mordecai Levy was described as 'glass-flowerer' of Whitechapel when declared a bankrupt in the *London Gazette* in 1770.
22. Bill formerly in the possession of the Newcastle Assembly Rooms.
23. H. Wakefield, *19th Century British Glass,* London (1961), p. 37 and Pl. 48B.
24. Sun Insurance policies Vol. 150, No. 220517, communicated by Miss N. Rothstein.
25. Printed on their trade-card, in the Banks Collection, British Museum Print Room (400219 (1817), Banks D. 2).
26. Barbara Morris, *Victorian Table Glass and Ornaments,* London (1978), p. 78, states that Robert Haddock appears in the local *Directories* as an engraver between 1827 and 1853. She also records Robert Pyle as an engraver, 1834-47.
27. Westropp, *op. cit.,* p. 199.
28. W. Buckley, 'Art Treasures Exhibition, IV. Glass' *Burlington Magazine,* LXI (1932), p. 178, Pl. VI, B. A rummer from this service was exhibited at Grosvenor House in 1976 by Alan Tillman (Antiques) Ltd. (*Country Life* (3 June, 1976), Supplement p. 52).
29. Sunderland Museum, *The Glass Industry of Tyne and Wear Part 1: Glassmaking on Wearside,* Gateshead (1979), p. 8. The author also records Thomas Bulmer as an engraver at this time.
30. R. J. Charleston, 'To Satyrize the Crispinites', *Glass Circle Paper,* No. 155, p. 5.
31. F. Buckley, *OEG,* p. 138, No. 85.
32. *Id.,* 'Notes on Glasshouses of Stourbridge', *l.c.,* p. 119. In 1767 he was shown as 'now or late of Stourbridge'.
33. *Id., OEG,* p. 140.

34. Victoria and Albert Museum, *Exhibition of English Glass, 1968, Catalogue,* No. 268, illustrated VAM *English Glass,* London (1968), fig. 62.
35. *Op. cit.,* pp. 37, 41.
36. Kindly communicated by Mrs. J. McNab Dennis.
37. I should like to express here my gratitude to Miss Pye for giving me access to her family's treasures.
38. I owe this reference to Mr. Donovan Dawe, formerly Principal Keeper, the Guildhall Library.
39. Manuscript temporarily deposited in the Ceramics Department, Victoria and Albert Museum, the property of Mr. Weston-Bird.
40. Manuscript in the possession of the Worshipful Company of Goldsmiths.
41. Illustrated Derek Davis, *English and Irish Antique Glass,* London (1964), fig. 65.
42. Hugh Wakefield, 'Glasswares at the Great Exhibition of 1851', *Annales du 7e Congrès de l'Association Internationale pour l'Histoire du Verre,* Liège (1978), p. 426.
43. I owe this information to Mr. Hugh Wakefield.
44. The subject is treated at greater length by our late member A. J. B. Kiddell, 'William Absolon Junior of Great Yarmouth', *Transactions of the English Ceramic Circle,* 5, Part 1 (1960), pp. 53-63.
45. H. Kühnert, *Urkundenbuch zur Thüringischen Glashüttengeschichte,* Jena (1934), p. 17.
46. See also John Harris *et al., Buckingham Palace,* London (1968), pp. 44, 46.
47. A. Graves, *The Society of Artists,* London (1907), p. 61.
48. D. R. Guttery, *From Broad Glass to Cut Crystal,* London (1956), p. 113.

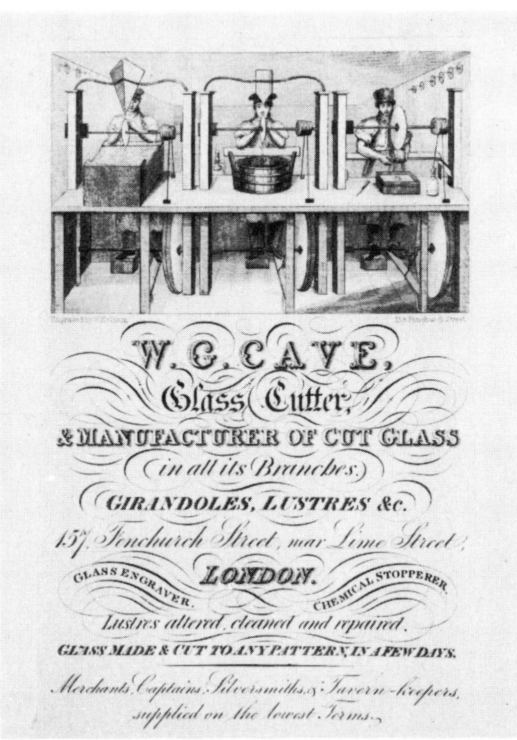

Figure 1. Trade-card of W. G. Cave, 157 Fenchurch Street, London, early 19th century. Guildhall Library, City of London.

Figure 2. Tumbler, cut and wheel-engraved by John Unsworth of Manchester, about 1800. H. $4\frac{1}{2}$in. (11. 5 cm.) Metropolitan Borough of Wigan.

Figure 3. Trade-card of John Unsworth, of Manchester, dated in ink '1792'. Trustees of the British Museum.

Figure 4. Tankard inscribed 'TYZACK Glass Maker'. Presumably Newcastle-on-Tyne, second half of 18th century. H. 6 in. (15. 2 cm.) Victoria and Albert Museum. Crown Copyright.

Figure 5. Jug, wheel-engraved with themes commemorating Lord Nelson, by John Williams of Newcastle-on-Tyne (see fig. 6). H. $6\frac{1}{4}$in. (16 cm.) Monmouth District Council. Photograph: Rex Moreton.

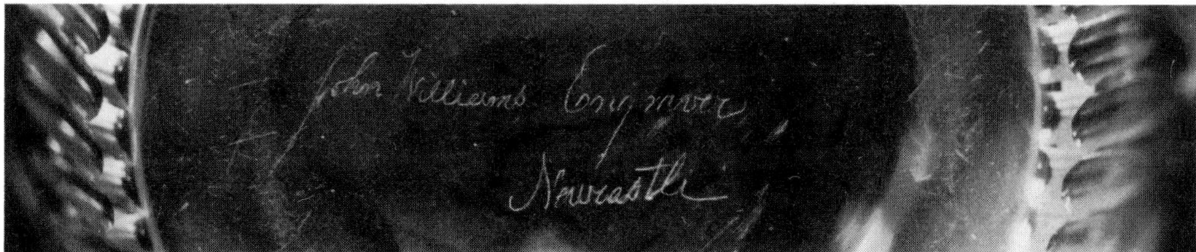

Figure 6. Signature in diamond-point on base of jug shown in fig. 5.

Figure 7. Claret-jug, cut and wheel-engraved by W. Herbert of Dudley, dated 1833. Signed 'W. Herbert'. H. 11⅝in. (29. 5 cm). Private collection. Victoria and Albert Museum photograph. Crown Copyright.

T. ILLIDGE & SON

Respectfully inform the MERCHANTS and MANUFACTURERS of (or in) Birmingham and its Vicinity, that they have commenced Business in the above Line, at No. 33, Cherry-street, nearly opposite the end of Cannon-street, where a great Variety of Specimens of Engravings and Etchings may be seen. ARMS, CRESTS, REGIMENTAL BADGES, rich and plain CYPHERS, FRUITS, FLOWERS, BORDERS, and FANCY DEVICES executed in a superior Manner. INDIA and all other SHADES, MOONS, and CHIMNEYS bordered or otherwise ornamented. LIQUOR BOTTLES, ACID BOTTLES, and CRUETS lettered and labelled. SMELLING BOTTLES screwed, and handsomely engraved. DRILLING. All Kinds of MEASURES for CHEMICAL and other PHILOSOPHICAL Purposes, graduated into any Number of equal Parts, Cubic Inches and their Decimals, or in any other Manner. The various MEASURES for the USE of APOTHECARIES, as ordered by the London Royal College of Physicians, kept for sale, or graduated and figured to order with the utmost Accuracy.

T. Illidge, sen. begs leave to add, that besides receiving particular Instructions from the late Mr. Timothy Lane, F.R.S. the Inventor of Apothecaries' Measures, he has been favoured with the following Testimonial from the Gentleman appointed by the College to edite their last Pharmacopœia.

> 'From my Intercourse with Mr. Lane, and the Communica-
> 'tions and Explanations which I had with him at the Time of
> 'the Adoption of his Division of Liquids by Measure or Bulk
> 'for Medical Use, I believe that the Principles adopted by Mr.
> 'Illidge, to be those which were applied in their original Forma-
> 'tion, and to afford the Means of obtaining correct Measures.
>
> 'R. POWELL, M.D.'

'Bedford Place, Dec. 24, 1816.'

It is T. Illidge, sen.'s Intention to spend much of his Time in Birmingham, personally to superintend the Execution of the Orders which they may be favoured with, and he trusts that the Quality of their Work, and their Punctuality and Dispatch of Business will merit their Approbation, and secure the Encouragement and Confidence of their Employers.

Letters addressed to T. I. and Son, either in London or Birmingham, will be duly attended to.

Figure 8. Advertisement of T. Illidge & Son, London and Birmingham, from Wrightson's *New Triennial Directory of Birmingham* (1818), pp. 72-3.

Figure 9. Jug, wheel-engraved with arms of the City of London by John Pye, London, about 1820-30. H. 8in. (20. 5 cm.). Private Collection. Copyright: Cecil Davis Ltd.

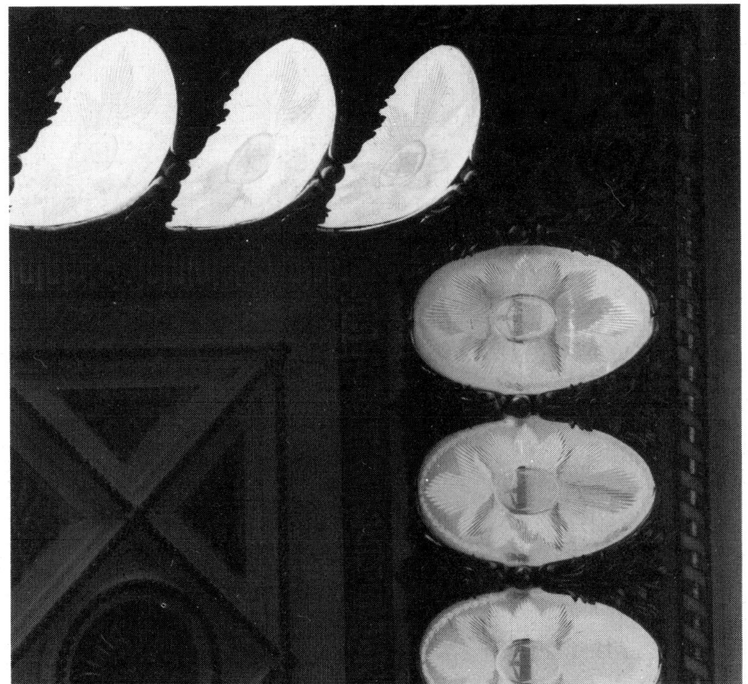

Figure 10. Skylight in the Guard Chamber, Buckingham Palace, wheel-engraved by Wainwright, about 1830. Reproduced by Gracious Permission of Her Majesty the Queen.

Figure 11. Plaque, wheel-engraved and signed 'Coles', early 19th century. D. app. 4in. (10 cm.) Private Collection. Victoria and Albert Museum photograph. Crown Copyright.

English Rock Crystal Glass 1878-1925

by IAN WOLFENDEN

A Paper read to the Circle on 19 May, 1977

'Ornament', wrote Ralph Wornum in 1851, 'is not a luxury, but, in a certain stage of the mind, an absolute necessity.'[1] This belief influenced industrial design in England through most of the Victorian period. Many Victorian styles were ornamental styles. They were also historical, and a basic problem for the Victorian designer was how to clothe the ornamental styles of the past in a contemporary dress. Owen Jones, in his *Examples of Chinese Ornament,* written in 1867, declared: 'I venture to hope that the publication of these types of . . . Ornament . . . will be found, by all those in the practice of Ornamental Art, a valuable aid in building up what we all seek,—the progressive development of the forms of the past, founded on the eternal principles which all good forms of Art display.' In Jones's view the best historical styles revealed the principles of ornament. Progress would be achieved by modifying the styles in accordance with the principles. Such ideas were widespread in the mid-nineteenth century, and glass, in common with other industrial arts, benefited from them. Rock crystal glass was rich in ornament, and it provides us with a notable example of the Victorian pursuit of artistic progress.

Technology furthered the development of ornament in all Victorian art industries. New manufacturing and decorative techniques flourished and there were revivals and improvements of traditional methods. The glass industry developed copper-wheel engraving so that, in the second half of the nineteenth century, it enjoyed a commercial success unprecedented in its history. Mostly this success was based upon long established practice, but rock crystal glass was an innovation. In simple terms 'rock crystal' was an engraved glass which had been wholly polished. In the best work the glass was thick and the engraving deep. The polish was obtained, as on cut glass, by the application of putty powder or, after about 1890, by immersion in acid.[2] The bright finish of the engraving stressed the relationship with cut glass and in much 'rock crystal' cut and engraved patterns were complementary. The term 'rock crystal' defined an engraving technique, but cut decoration formed the basis of many styles of rock crystal work. Traditionally, English engraving had been pictorial, inscriptional or heraldic, and its predominantly matt texture contrasted with a bright glass ground. Rock crystal glass, through polished engraving, cutting and sometimes etching, achieved more varied effects. These were occasionally derived from oriental jade or rock crystal carvings, which were one source of inspiration for the new technique.

English rock crystal glass was primarily the work of West Midlands factories. In the Victorian period the West Midlands, in particular the Stourbridge area, gradually assumed leadership in tableglass design. During the third quarter of the nineteenth century Stourbridge became a major influence on English engraving. In the 1850s and early 1860s, as engraving became increasingly fashionable, some of the best English work was done to the order of London retailers. The retailers produced designs for blanks supplied from outside and had them engraved locally. Sometimes the blanks were sent from Stourbridge.[3] By the 1870s the Stourbridge firms themselves were designing and engraving glass of high quality. At this period Central European engravers, immigrating in small but decisive numbers, were settling in various British glass centres. In Stourbridge, Thomas Webb and Sons took on two Bohemians, Frederick E. Kny and William Fritsche, to run engraving workshops. At the Paris International Exhibition of 1878 Webb's gained the Grand Prix chiefly for their engraved glass.[4]

The presence of Bohemian engravers in Stourbridge in the 1870s greatly facilitated the introduction of rock crystal glass. Deep engraving, characteristic of rock crystal work, was traditional in Bohemia. It had been admired, but not imitated in England at least since the 1840s. With Bohemian craftsmen at their disposal the Stourbridge factories of the late nineteenth century were now capable of engraving deeply on thick glass, and the technical foundations of English rock crystal were laid chiefly by the firm of Thomas Webb. On Webb's glass shown at the Paris International Exhibition in 1878 the *Art Journal* had these comments: 'Another development is that of deep, bright cutting, sometimes in relief, like a cameo, sometimes sunk, as in intaglio; in either case thick glass is employed and the deepest portions are sunk to the depth of an inch or more. This method has been adopted with great effect both by the French and English manufacturers and engravers. . . . Our own countrymen have largely employed figure subjects, generally taking them from the antique. In Messrs. Webb's collection is a portion of the frieze of the Parthenon, executed in relief and polished, producing an object of truly high Art.'[5]

A vase signed by Frederick Kny, now in a private collection, indicates the type of glass shown by Webb's in Paris in 1878 (fig. 1). Figures derived from the Parthenon sculptures are engraved around the body of the vase in high relief. The figures have received a light, irregular polish. Kny's glass is presumably modelled upon the Elgin Vase of John Northwood, finished in 1873 and now in the Birmingham City Art Gallery; its date should be c. 1875-78. Its type represents what seemed in 1878 the distinctive English contribution to the new deep and polished engraving.

The *Art Journal* account of the engraved glass shown at the Paris Exhibition is interesting for several reasons. The term 'rock crystal' is not used anywhere but certainly the deep, bright engraving 'sunk, as in intaglio' was done in what we should call rock crystal technique. Apparently the French produced most of this sunk work and, in this respect, may have influenced the early development of English rock crystal. The English relief engraving, on the other hand, is given a prominence in the *Art Journal* commentary which its influence scarcely merits. It is now clear that at the 1878 Paris Exhibition the fashion for glass with figures after the antique effectively ended, whether these were sunk or in relief. The mid-1870s are a watershed in English glass design, at least as far as engraved glass is concerned, and the introduction of the rock crystal technique is one sign of the onset of the Late Victorian period. As early as 1851 Owen Jones had said: 'Here, in Europe, we have been studying drawing from the human figure, but it has not led us forward in the art of ornamental design. Although the study of the human figure is useful in refining the taste . . . it is a roundabout way of learning to draw for the designer for manufactures.'[6] Nevertheless much mid-Victorian design was based upon the human figure. Renaissance and Greek art provided the main sources, and in engraved glass the Greek Revival or 'Grecian' style was pre-eminent from about 1850 until the early 1870s. Those pages of the Webb factory pattern books which may be dated to the early 1870s bear charmingly naive drawings for engraved glass, with figures derived from Greek vase paintings or the sculptures of the Parthenon. By 1878 Grecian designs scarcely appear. The new rock crystal technique was accompanied by new styles, which often had their entire basis in ornamental design and rarely employed the human figure.

The chief impulse towards fresh, predominantly ornamental styles came from Oriental art. Webb patterns and those of Stevens and Williams of Brierley Hill show Oriental influence by the mid-1870s, and some of the English engraved glass shown at the Vienna Universal Exhibition of 1873 had a Japanese or Chinese flavour.[7] An account of the glass exhibited in Vienna by Pellatt and Co. and Pellatt and Wood of London noted: 'an infusion of Japanese art which is steadily moving into European designs was apparent in a very charming service with engraved panels in which were storks and vases with plants, and the conventional key bands and scrolls of Japan work . . . reminded the observer of some of the highest qualities of Chinese engraving on pure rock crystal.'[8] There is no indication that this English engraving of 1873 was either polished or deep. Nevertheless it may have influenced the earliest French deep, polished work, which was apparently that shown in Paris in 1878. Of this French glass the *Art Journal* noted: 'Our neighbours . . . have adopted some square and rhomboidal forms similar to those often employed by the Chinese and Japanese potters and have produced bold floral patterns with birds and other objects in this deep engraving, which is brilliantly polished.'[9] In particular the use of natural rock crystal by the Chinese and the floral and other motifs of Japanese art were important for the development of a rock crystal glass.

However, these Oriental influences did not wholly determine the styles of English rock crystal. Possibly the first piece of English rock crystal glass was a silver-mounted claret jug in Celtic style, shown by Thomas Webb and Sons in Paris in 1878 (fig. 2). It was described in 1885 as: 'purchased . . . at the Paris Exhibition, 1878. Partly etched with acid and then engraved in detail . . . and polished with very small wheels.'[10] The jug is not described as 'rock crystal' but the technical description allies it both to the French deep engraved glass of 1878 and to the earliest documented English rock crystal glass. Almost certainly the jug was designed by J. M. O'Fallon, who wrote the 1885 description and who was Webb's Art Director for the Paris Exhibition.[11] The use of the Celtic style, with its rich interlace work, is indicative of the growing interest in ornamental as opposed to figurative design. But as an individual style the Celtic could not compete with the Oriental styles, which were easier to execute, and it did not long survive.

On the evidence of the mounted claret jug it seems reasonable to credit J. M. O'Fallon with the introduction of English rock crystal glass in the early months of 1878. There is support for this view in the manuscript 'Reminiscences Industrial' of the Webb cameo carver, Tom Woodall. Woodall's 'Reminiscences' were written in 1912, and the simplest interpretation of the following passage from them would suggest O'Fallon as the originator of 'rock crystal': 'We had a good run (sc. in cameo glass) but had to follow up in ordinary Flint work mostly engravings and 'Rock crystal' or Intaglio which was polished by cutters and eventually by acid. I would like to say that the first intaglio was designed by O'Fallon who was chief designer for the firm for the Paris 1878 Exhibition and was some intaglio exhibited there executed by cutters but was eventually done on special lathes.'[12] The 'intaglio' technique is quite different from 'rock crystal' and originated in about 1890.[13] If we allow for Woodall's later confusion of the two techniques we may accept that he associates O'Fallon with the introduction of rock crystal work.

The earliest extant record of the term 'rock crystal' is in the Webb factory pattern books, dated 6th July, 1878.[14] A group of three patterns bears the note 'Engraved as Rock Crystal (Kny)' and the date. The first two patterns are for tankards, the third for a jug (fig. 3). Drawn in a naturalistic manner the tankard designs are of fish among rushes, the jug design of owls. At this date no other English firm seems to have been producing rock crystal work. The earliest known glass is in the Webb factory collection, a wineglass with an engraved acanthus scroll and monogram, of August 1878.[15] Brush polished and slightly matt in texture, the engraving is fairly shallow on thin glass. The delicate acanthus scroll is in a Renaissance manner, and the glass has the appearance of a transitional piece (fig. 4). In 1878 there was an experimental air about Webb's rock crystal glass but the technique quickly became established. Following its introduction matt engraving declined in Stourbridge and Brierly Hill. For the next twenty five years or so the major firms of Webb and Stevens and Williams made little engraved glass other than rock crystal. A Stourbridge publication of 1903 noted: 'Polished rock crystal may be named among the styles in which delightfully rich effects are produced. The old style of engraving was one in which a dulled appearance was in fashion but in the present there is a strong contrast to this in the bright finish that is in vogue.'[16]

Analysis of the broad development of English rock crystal from its tentative beginnings in 1878 to its culmination in the early years of the twentieth century reveals several basic features. First, there is the combination of cutting with engraving, natural on the thick glass. The favourite cut motifs are the flute and the pillar. Both these motifs were popular in the Victorian period, particularly in its early phase. The pillar was an Early Victorian speciality, developing from the Regency pillared flute under the influence of Bohemian glass of the Biedermeier period. Pillars are slightly convex panels, framed by mitre cuts which usually form a rounded arch at the top of the panel. The mitre cuts are smoothed, or 'pillared', along their whole length. On early rock crystal glass up to about 1885 the pillars are most often vertical and arranged in series around the bowl or body of a vessel (fig. 5).[17] Flutes tend to accompany the pillars on stems or necks. From the mid-1880s, particularly on Webb glass, the pillars often assume a curved form (fig. 6).[18] During the 1890s, again particularly on Webb glass, the pillars may twist through the whole form of a glass in a serpentine line, losing their arches and, on stems at least, becoming much thinner.[19] The flute, which tends to remain vertical, consequently diminishes in importance.

The basis of much rock crystal work, the table-services in particular, is therefore the cut pillar. Grafted on to the pillar work is engraving in a variety of ornamental styles. These styles, in the best rock crystal glass, are usually new to glass engraving. Rock crystal glass is in large measure an amalgam of essentially Early Victorian cutting and Late Victorian engraved ornament. It is not therefore Revivalist or Historicist as was the Grecian engraved glass of the 1850s to 1870s. It is worked in a new manner, which may now be considered in more detail.

The first rock crystal patterns, as noted above, are of fish and owls in a naturalistic style. These were the work of Frederick Kny, who had previously carried out much figure work for Webb's, particularly in the Grecian style.[20] Kny tended to specialize in birds and other animals and in the human figure. He was expert in figurative work in the Mid-Victorian manner. Thus, although he did accept the Late Victorian ornamental styles fostered by rock crystal, he seems where possible to have employed figure designs in the new technique. A fine example is the 'Hunting the Eagle' decanter, now in the Victoria and Albert Museum (fig. 7).[21] This is engraved in an essentially naturalistic style and shows *putti* hunting eagles amid intertwined oak and ivy branches. The design is apparently adapted from that on a silver salver by Christesen's of Denmark, shown in the Paris Exhibition of 1878.[22] Kny has substituted eagles, a favourite subject of his, for a boar on the salver; an eagle and oak branches also feature on a design for a matt engraved jug produced by Kny in about 1865.[23] The 'Hunting the Eagle' glass may be dated c. 1878-80, although it is traditionally given as c. 1890.

The style of Kny's 'Hunting the Eagle' decanter is conservative for the late 1870s. Nevertheless, naturalistic ornament is significant in early rock crystal glass. On Webb glass it usually takes the form of flowers and birds engraved on simple pillars. Examples date from 1880-81.[24] Much contemporary work by the Stevens and Williams factory is also of this type, but the style is more distinctly Japanese. Japanese floral and bird designs had featured on the French deep engraved glass at Paris in 1878. Stevens and Williams exploited the commercial possibilities of this naturalistic Japanese work on their rock crystal glass from 1879 until 1885 and sometimes beyond. The first reference in the Stevens and Williams pattern books to polished engraving is in November, 1879; the design is in Japanese style.[25] A glass of December 1879 survives in the factory collection (fig. 8).[26] This champagne is brush polished and slightly matt like the earliest known Webb glass of 1878. Japanese floral work is engraved freely across unemphatic vertical cuts in a fashion adopted for other Stevens and Williams rock crystal. A jug of 1884 in the factory collection (fig. 9) and a decanter of 1885 in the Dudley Art Gallery both have freely arranged engraved ornament in the Japanese manner.[27] At least some of this Japanese ornament was designed for Stevens and Williams by a freelance Bohemian designer and engraver, Joseph Keller. The design for the 1879 champagne, for example, is found in Keller's Design Book.[28] However, the extent of Keller's contribution to early rock crystal designs is uncertain; the actual engraving was almost always done in the factory workshop. In charge of the shop at this period was a man named Miller or Millar, who was possibly of Bohemian extraction; the slang term 'millrock' is still remembered in the factory for his rock crystal glass.[29]

Japanese designs were commonly chosen for their naturalistic element. Stevens and Williams' glass in this style may be regarded as the equivalent of Webb glass decorated with a European flora and fauna. The whole development, beginning with matt work of about 1873, was in reaction to the formalities of the Grecian style. A further reaction occurred in about 1883, when rock crystal glass, at Webb's in particular, became increasingly ornamental. Stylized designs replaced naturalistic. Above all, the basis of the new work was stylized floral ornament, especially as derived from Chinese art. One of the most spectacular pieces in the new style was the bowl designed by John Northwood and made by Stevens and Williams for the International Health Exhibition in 1884 (fig. 10).[30] The ornament was probably copied from plate LXXXV of Owen Jones's *Examples of Chinese Ornament*.

Jones's book was particularly influential on Webb glass of the years 1883-90. *Examples of Chinese Ornament* offered a recantation of Jones's earlier view of Chinese art, expressed in his *Grammar of Ornament* of 1856. There Jones had said: 'If we go to nature as the Egyptians and Greeks went, we may hope; but if we go there like the Chinese . . . we should gain but little.' When he wrote his *Grammar* Jones had little knowledge of the conventional forms of Chinese ornament but by 1867, the date of the *Examples*, his awareness of Chinese art was much fuller. He became convinced that Chinese ornamental forms could provide the basis of an industrial art style. Thus the *Examples* illustrated designs for cloisonné enamel work, where the technique tended to impose stylization. Such designs were adopted by Webb's for their rock crystal glass, in two distinct manners. Sometimes the form of the glass itself might appear Chinese and the ornament therefore wholly in sympathy; sometimes the ornament was grafted on to a pillar type glass with a resulting 'Anglo-Chinese' effect.[31] A glass to a pattern of 1883, recently acquired by the Pilkington Glass Museum, is an example of the former method (fig. 12).[32] A sherry and a hock of 1884 and 1889 respectively will serve to show the Anglo-Chinese style (fig. 11).[33]

The sherry and hock in question are both in the Webb factory collection. Both have Chinese-style floral ornament engraved on cut pillars of ogival shape. The pillars are alternately upright and reversed. Plate XLIX of Jones's *Examples of Chinese Ornament* gives a range of flower designs from which the ornament was apparently adopted. The round funnel bowls, baluster stems and fluted knops of both glasses are thoroughly Victorian. Yet this mixture is undoubtedly successful. The reason lies in the ease with which the Chinese patterns could be rendered in the copper-wheel engraving technique. Simple ball cuts and edge cuts render the peculiar scrolled forms of the Chinese-style leaves. Similar cuts fringe the pillars and echo the main ornament. A unity of style is thus achieved through attention to technique. One is reminded of Owen Jones's thirteenth proposition of his *Grammar of Ornament:* 'Flowers, or other natural objects, should not be used as ornaments; but conventional representations founded upon them, sufficiently suggestive to convey the intended image to the mind, without destroying the unity of the object they are employed to decorate.' Jones, and also Matthew Digby Wyatt, had praised the qualities of stylized Oriental ornament since the early 1850s. Webb's Anglo-Chinese glass is a fine example of where their theories and example could lead.

Economy of technique is perhaps the main reason for this change in style from naturalistic to conventional in the early 1880s at Webb's. Not only rock crystal glass but cameo work assumed a Chinese appearance for a while. The effect was to reduce still further the opportunities for animal or human figure work, already decreasing under the Japanese influence of the late 1870s. The basic concern was to abandon the concept of engraving as a 'picture on the glass' in the interests of unity of design. In some of their art glass of the 1880s Webb's further developed the relationship between form and decoration. A series of designs for vases and bowls decorated with fish amid waves integrated the cut and the engraved work so closely that the distinction between the techniques disappears. The vessels date from 1885 to 1890 and reproduce the effect of carved Oriental vases. One bowl, dating from 1890, is attributed in the factory pattern books to George Woodall, the cameo carver.[34] The finest glass of the series is perhaps the twelve-inch vase now in a private collection (fig. 13).[35] In this glass of 1889 fish are scattered across the surface like fossils in a bed of rock. The design has a unity reminiscent of the moulded glass of René Lalique. Such Webb art glass, and the tableware in Chinese style, all dating from the 1880s, are perhaps the most successful of all rock crystal glass types. In a typically Victorian manner they combine technical innovation with rich ornamental and formal design.

Fashions changed rapidly in Late Victorian glass. Between 1880 and 1900 Webb's alone created approximately 13,000 new patterns, an average of over ten per week. In assessing the most significant development in rock crystal glass of the later 1880s and the 1890s it is useful to concentrate for a while upon the work of the finest of the rock crystal engravers, William Fritsche of Thomas Webb and Sons. Fritsche's work is traceable through the fairly large number of patterns ascribed to him in the factory pattern and price books. From these it is clear that his style came to maturity in the period from about 1884 to the early 1890s, and there is good reason to believe that this style was in large measure personal to him.[36] It should also be noted here that at this date Stevens and Williams were producing less advanced work and that during the 1890s they made only a small quantity of rock crystal glass.

The style of William Fritsche may first be studied in his most remarkable work, the ewer now in the Corning Museum of Glass in the U.S.A. The ewer is signed, 'W. Fritsche Stourbridge 1886' (fig. 14).[37] It is an example of what the Victorians termed 'High Art', an art which, in the words of John Stewart, 'appeals not to the eye only, but to the mind of the spectator'.[38] This description of the ewer in a contemporary pamphlet amplifies the point: 'The whole ewer may be said to represent the progress of a river from its birth in a rocky hillside till it loses itself at last in the blue infinity of the sea. The neck of the ewer represents the mountain birth-place of the stream . . . On the front of the neck is carved, in very bold relief, the beautiful head of the water god himself, garlanded with rushes and aquatic plants, and with his curling beard flowing into the stream of clear water beneath. . . . The rush and hurry of the rapid river are wonderfully expressed by the strong, clear, curving volutes of the body of the ewer. . . . The lowest part of the body of the ewer is formed of a great fluted shell, which is symbolical of the bottom of the sea. . . . The decoration of the foot is a bold treatment of shells and weeds, from which rises a water spout or sudden upheaval of the waters of the ocean, thus forming the pedestal, and consistently carrying out the artist's idea.'[39]

In essence the Corning ewer is a work of narrative sculpture. In working it Fritsche brought into focus certain technical and stylistic preoccupations of the mid 1880s. The upper parts of the body are cut pillar work, mingling with the deeply engraved areas above and below as elements in a single design. A powerful rhythm, reminiscent of Baroque art, informs the whole vessel. Occasionally a lighter, flickering scrollwork suggests the Rococo. All parts of the ewer are subject to the narrative theme, which demands a reading from top to bottom, from river source to sea-bed. Narrative elements, other than in such a 'High Art' glass, are rare in 'rock crystal'. However, the swirling lines of mixed cut and engraved work are not uncommon in Fritsche's tableservice designs of this period, which develop gradually towards a Rococo Revival in the 1890s.

The lip of the Corning ewer is notable for its restless outline and its tight scrolls. These features, coupled with the strong sense of movement in the whole glass, are typical of William Fritsche's best rock crystal work. Restlessness is perhaps the dominant characteristic. Fritsche regularly visited his Bohemian homeland and perhaps there became aware of the deep engraved Baroque and Rococo glass of Silesia, which shares this character.[40] The curved pillars and tight scrolls feature on Fritsche's glass as early as 1881, in a tableservice with lizards engraved along the edge of the pillared cuts (fig. 15).[41] The full sense of movement is seen in several designs of 1886 and is still found in a service of 1897 (fig. 17).[42] The 1897 service illustrates Fritsche's cavalier treatment of the pillar style in certain of his designs of the 1890s. The pillars in this instance take the form of the 'Indian Pine', a textile motif discussed and admired by design reformers such as Ralph Wornum and Owen Jones since the 1850s. Set free in a swirling design so beloved of Fritsche, the pillar has lost its traditional function of stabilizing and articulating the ornament. In the stemmed vessels from this service the restlessness is further expressed by thin, twisting pillars which curve from the foot-rim to the lower part of the bowl.

Fritsche's ornament of this type may perhaps be termed, from its major motifs, 'scroll and pillar' work. It is extravagant and unrestrained and it represents the most thoroughly Bohemian contribution to English engraving made by the immigrants of the later nineteenth century. Comparable in their richness are the designs of F. Kretschmann, a Bohemian who worked for Webb's in the late 1880s. Kretschmann is found in the *Stourbridge Almanack and Directory* as a glass engraver living in Wollaston from 1886 to 1892. This may well be the period during which he worked for Webb's. His designs, which are not common, suggest a predilection for heavy, symmetrical forms, sometimes of Renaissance inspiration (fig. 16). He made use of tight scrollwork and, occasionally, of the Chinese ornament popular in the 1880s.[43] There is insufficient evidence to clarify his design relationship to Fritsche but he worked deep in the glass and was undoubtedly a kindred spirit.

Note has been made of a Rococo element in the glass of William Fritsche in the 1880s. This was a significant feature, for by the late 1880s Webb's were on the verge of a Rococo Revival. A Fritsche design of June, 1889, is an early example of the style. The pattern is for a clareteen with Rococo C-scroll and diaper work.[44] Tightly packed flowers and leafy scrolls enrich the design in the manner of the 'scroll and pillar' work. In the 1890s the ornament is reduced to more strictly Revivalist motifs and the total effect simplified. A decanter of 1894, now in the Merseyside County Museums, may be taken as an example (fig. 18).[45] The glass is thin except for the lower part of the body, which is pillar moulded. Above this there is shallow engraved Rococo-style decoration. Such a glass was cheaper to produce than the deeply cut and engraved work typical of the 1880s, and there seems little doubt that economic motives were in part responsible for the introduction of the new style. Both Webb's and Stevens and Williams seem to have faced financial problems around 1890. From John Northwood II's biography of his father we learn that the costly cameo glass technique was virtually abandoned in about 1890 in favour of the cheaper intaglio process. Similarly, Webb's made increasing use from this date of moulding techniques on their rock crystal glass. They also tended to employ thinner glass. However, a further impulse towards a new style may well have been the success of Rococo enamelled work produced for Webb's in the early 1890s by the Frenchman, Jules Barbe.[46] Barbe did many designs in a Rococo Revival manner at this date and they are closely related to rock crystal work in rococo style. A sherry in rock crystal technique by Fritsche, dated 1894, shows Rococo ornament on the bowl above a twist pillared stem (fig. 19).[47] Although overlapping with other styles in the 1890s the Rococo Revival predominates in Webb rock crystal work at this period.

The re-introduction of an historical style marks the beginning of the decline of the rock crystal technique. The decline may be observed partly in technical factors such as shallower engraving and thinner glass and partly in a decrease in originality of design. Above all, the revival of Historicism perhaps inevitably led to the return of matt engraving, since the historical styles had originally been rendered in the matt technique. At Webb's there was still little matt engraved glass in the 1890s, when the Rococo style was predominant. However, in the early years of the twentieth century the Rococo was gradually replaced by Neo-classical styles for which matt work came increasingly to be used to offset the polished engraving. Edwardian Neo-classic glass was probably a reaction to the Art Nouveau style, which appears in rock crystal glass chiefly at Stevens and Williams. Garlands in the Neo-classic manner are found on Webb rock crystal as early as 1889, but the style reaches its height only c. 1900-1910.[48] As late as 1907 deep and wholly polished work in Neo-classic style occurs at Webb's, as on a tumbler and liqueur in the factory collection.[49] After this date there is usually some matt work accompanying the polished; the term 'rock crystal' is used less and less and by 1908-09 it is doubtful if the term should be applied to any of the polished work still being done. 'Engraved bright' is now normal factory usage. Some pretty designs of 1912, with parrots and garlands, illustrate the type. A bowl and sherry with these motifs are in the Dudley Art Gallery collections (fig. 20).[50] An exquisite tall wine in the Webb factory collection, signed by Fritsche, has engraved rose garlands, now largely matt.[51] This also dates from 1912 and is very far removed from Fritsche's rock crystal glass of the 1880s.

By about 1900 other firms in the Stourbridge area were producing rock crystal glass. L. and S. Hingley showed 'rock crystal' in London in 1908 and both Stuart and Sons and Webb Corbett have series of rock crystal work recorded in their pattern books for the early 1900s.[52] Surviving glass in the factory collections of Stuart's and Webb Corbett does not suggest that either firm made much of high quality. The best rock crystal glass of these final years of the technique was almost certainly that of Stevens and Williams of Brierley Hill. This firm specialized for a few years in work in the Art Nouveau style. The designer Frederick Carder, who left for America in 1903, was probably responsible for many of the Art Nouveau patterns, which were executed in the factory workshop under the direction of John Orchard. Some of the glass simply has Art Nouveau motifs applied to a body cut in pillar style. A puff box of 1900 in the Victoria and Albert Museum (fig. 21) and an inkwell in the factory collection, dating from 1902, illustrate the manner (fig. 22).[53] In a tumbler of 1901 in the factory collection the spirit of Art Nouveau is captured far more successfully (fig. 24).[54] A series of pillarintas, or small pillars, around the base of the tumbler form the basis for a flowing line that rises through the glass like a cold flame. A fine decanter of 1903, now in a private collection, has deep, sinuous cutting and rich floral work of Art Nouveau type (fig. 23).[55] The pattern for this glass is dated June, 1903 and may represent an alternative to Carder's more orthodox versions of the style. Certainly the decanter is in some respects reminiscent of Webb's rock crystal of the 1880s and 1890s, although the detail is undoubtedly Art Nouveau. Originating in 1898, Stevens and Williams' Art Nouveau is in decline by 1905-1906. As at Webb's, the rock crystal technique is scarcely recorded in the pattern books from 1907. However, it does survive the First World War; a series of vases of 1923 were engraved by or under H. Whitworth in Japanese flower and bird style, for Stevens and Williams. The commercial limit of the technique was reached quite early in the Edwardian period.

In attempting to assess the contribution of 'rock crystal' to the glass history of the late nineteenth century the complexity of the period must be borne in mind. Rock crystal glass was one of a large number of new types of glass introduced at that time. However, it may be suggested that, as a major innovation in glass engraving, rock crystal glass is indicative of Late Victorian attitudes. In engraved glass the final quarter of the nineteenth century is marked by a shift from figurative to ornamental work. The Stourbridge factories developed styles of conventional ornament in some of their rock crystal glass which reflected possibly the theories and certainly the example of the design reformers of the mid-century. This may be interpreted as a move away from an historicist approach, in which specific historical styles were accorded a partisan favour, to one concerned with principles and the development of original styles of ornament. In place of the respect granted the Grecian style a range of oriental styles—Chinese, Japanese, Indian and Persian—were employed and modified. The words of John Stewart, writing in the *Art Journal* in 1862, no longer applied to the glass engravers of the rock crystal period: '. . . the productions of the best, and, indeed, of nearly all the British makers, have attained high success in purely Grecian forms . . .'[56] From the mid-1870s a greater breadth of outlook is apparent. We seem to move from the Mid to the Late Victorian era.

Perhaps because of this wider outlook the Late Victorian period offered greater opportunities for individual expression. The work of William Fritsche, the most talented of the Late Victorian engravers, is original and personal. The 'scroll and pillar' work, which roughly defines the restless manner frequently associated with Fritsche in the Webb pattern books, is a treatment of glass unique in English glass history. In the Corning ewer Fritsche produced perhaps the most powerful 'High Art' glass of the Victorian period. Nevertheless, individuals were rarely allowed public credit for their work. Rock crystal glass was a factory, not an individual, product. It emerged at a time of intense competition between factories, fostered by the great international exhibitions of the day. Originating in the year of the Paris International Exhibition of 1878 rock crystal glass declined as such exhibitions became less important in the early twentieth century. Increasingly too the factories abandoned the dangerous path of innovation. Traditional cut glass patterns exerted a growing influence. In rock crystal glass we see the last great example of English factory engraving.

NOTES

1. R.N.Wornum, 'The Exhibition as a Lesson in Taste', in the *Art Journal Illustrated Catalogue of the Industry of All Nations,* London (1851), p. XXI.***
2. Webb pattern book V. Note by pattern 17723 ('first large piece polished by acid'). July, 1889.
3. See, for instance, the glass exhibited by Messrs. W. and G. Phillips at the International Exhibition of 1862 (*Art Journal Illustrated Catalogue of the International Exhibition,* London (1862), p. 164).
4. J. M. O'Fallon, 'Glass engraving as an Art', in the *Art Journal* for 1885, London (1885), p. 313.
5. The *Art Journal Illustrated Catalogue of the Paris International Exhibition 1878,* London (1879), p. 144.
6. Quoted by John Stewart, 'The International Exhibition—its Influences and Results', in the *Art Journal Illustrated Catalogue of the International Exhibition,* London (1862), p. 32-33.
7. Webb pattern book L. See, e.g., patterns 8729, 8765 datable perhaps c.1873-74. Stevens and Williams description book 3. See, e.g., pattern 4390. The book dates from 1875 to 1877.
8. Prof. T. C. Archer, 'Report of the Manufactures of Glass, including Enamels', in *Reports on the Vienna Universal Exhibition of 1873,* pt. III, London, H.M.S.O. (1874), p. 173.
9. As reference (5).
10. J. M. O'Fallon, *op. cit.* in *n.* 4, p. 312.
11. It is noted in the *Art Journal Paris Catalogue* (*ibid.,* p. 137) that 'Messrs. Webb's Art manager, Mr. O'Fallon, has produced admirable examples in Gothic and Celtic styles'.
12. MS in the possession of Mrs. Wilday Allin.
13. 'Intaglio', in the sense recognised in Stourbridge, is an underhand grinding process, like engraving, done on stone wheels, as in cutting.
14. Webb pattern book 0. Patterns 10991, 10992 and 10993.
15. Dudley Art Gallery Exhibition Catalogue *English Rock Crystal Glass 1878-1925* (1976), no. 11 (hereafter referred to as *ERC*).
16. *The Black Country and its Industries,* No. 1, Stourbridge, Mark and Moody (1903), p. 6.
17. Webb pattern book Q. See, e.g., pattern 13175, datable to 1881.
18. Webb pattern book S. See, e.g., pattern 14276, dated 1883.
19. Webb pattern book X. See, e.g., pattern A 12, datable to 1892-1893.
20. Webb pattern book J. See, e.g., patterns 7303, 7377, datable to the late 1860s.
21. *ERC,* no. 14.
22. *The Art Journal Paris Catalogue, op. cit.* in *n.* 5, London (1878), p. 32.
23. Webb pattern book J. Pattern 6932.
24. Webb pattern book Q. See, e.g., pattern 13175, datable to 1881.
25. Stevens and Williams description book 4. Pattern 5689, engraved by Millar.
26. *ERC,* no. 51.
27. *ERC,* nos. 53 and 58 respectively.
28. *A collection of patterns for the use of Glass Decorators designed by Joseph Keller* (n.d.), fol. 237. The book is in the possession of the Dudley Art Gallery.
29. Information kindly supplied by Mr. Tom Jones, Designer for Royal Brierley Crystal.
30. *ERC,* no. 56.
31. Examples of forms influenced by Chinese bronzes occur as late as 1889. See Webb pattern book V, patterns 17365 ff, dated March, 1889.
32. The pattern for this glass is Webb 14072 in book S. There are slight differences between the glass and the pattern.
33. *ERC,* nos. 17 and 19 respectively.
34. *ERC,* no. 21.
35. *ERC,* no. 20.
36. Alfred S. Johnston, 'The Fritsche Ewer', typescript dated 1886 in the Webb factory files. Johnston notes: 'Mr. Fritsche generally designs his own work.'
37. *ERC,* no. 18a.
38. J. Stewart, *op. cit.* in *n.* 6, p. 95.
39. Alfred S. Johnston, *op. cit.* in *n.* 36.
40. For Fritsche's visits to Bohemia, see his obituary in the *Stourbridge County Advertiser,* 29 March, 1924.
41. Webb pattern book R. Pattern 13380.
42. Webb pattern book U. See, e.g., patterns 15625, 15887. *ERC,* no. 33.
43. For the use of scrollwork see Webb patternbook V, pattern 17457, dated 1889. Also in book V (pattern 16613) is a jug with Chinese ornament, dated 1888.
44. Webb pattern book V. Pattern 17681.
45. *ERC,* no. 31.
46. Webb pattern book W. See, e.g., patterns 18625, 18559.
47. *ERC,* no. 30.
48. For the early pattern see Webb pattern book W, pattern 18021.
49. *ERC,* nos. 36 and 37.
50. *ERC,* nos. 47 and 48.
51. The pattern is in Webb pattern book 1, no. 34934.
52. For Hingley's rock crystal glass see *The Pottery Gazette,* October, 1898, p. 1246. I am grateful to C. R. Hajdamach for this reference.
53. *ERC,* nos. 67 and 69 respectively.
54. *ERC,* no. 68.
55. *ERC,* no. 71.
56. J. Stewart, *op. cit.* in *n.* 6, p. 112.

PHOTOGRAPHIC ACKNOWLEDGEMENTS

Thanks are due to David Griffiths for the photographs, with the exception of the following: Corning Museum of Glass, New York (fig. 14), Christine Hajdamach (figs. 7, 18 and 24), Phillips Auctioneers, London (fig. 1) and the Victoria and Albert Museum (figs. 10 and 21).

Figure 1. Vase, matt engraved by F. E. Kny. Thomas Webb and Sons, Stourbridge, c. 1875. H. $7^{9}/_{16}$in. (19.2 cm.). Private Collection.

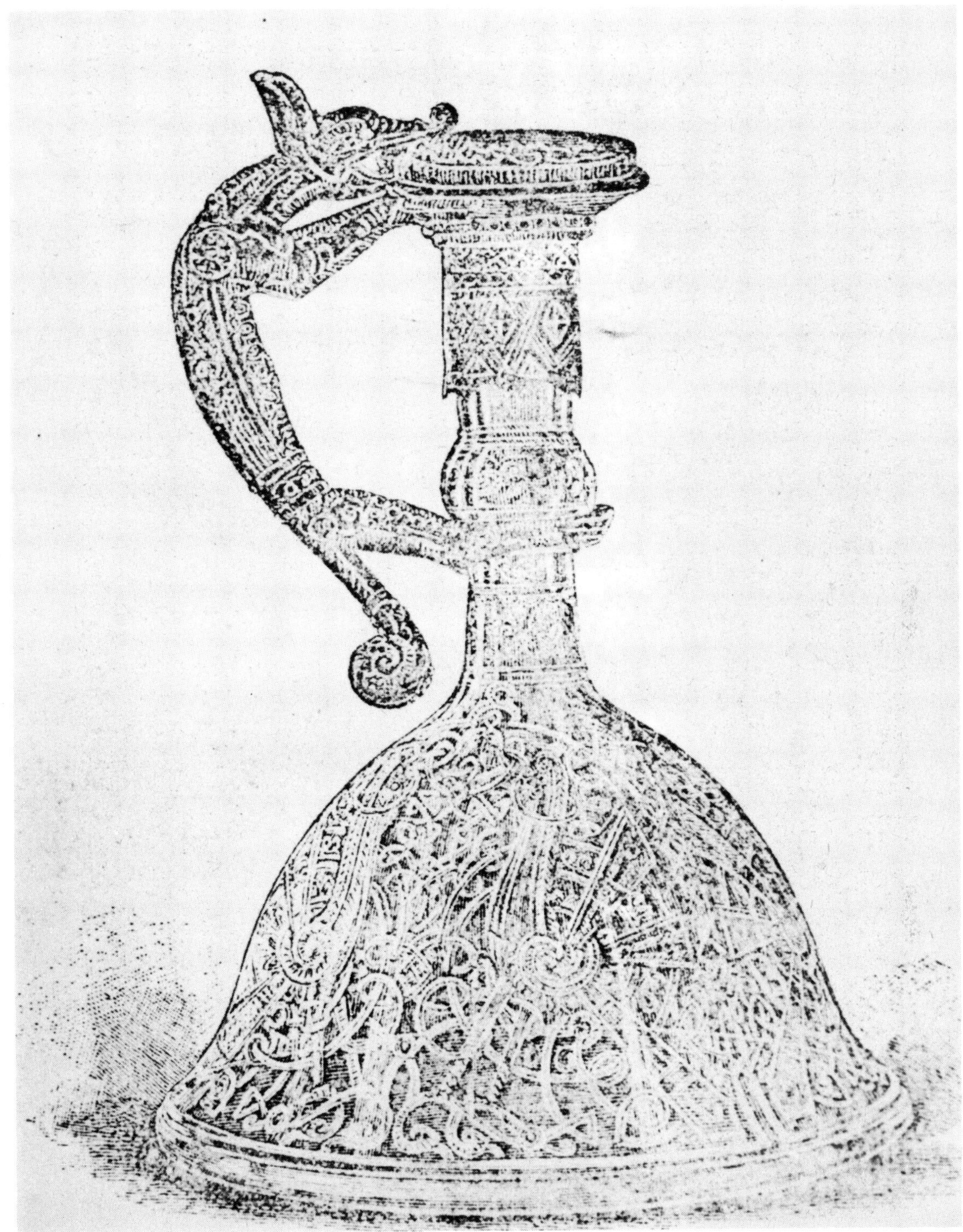

Figure 2. Claret jug with polished engraving. Illustration from the *Art Journal* (1885), p. 311, fig. 5.

Figure 3. Drawing for jug, rock crystal engraved by F. E. Kny. Thomas Webb and Sons, Stourbridge, pattern 10993, 1878. Dema Glass Ltd.

Figure 4. Wineglass, rock crystal engraved. Thomas Webb and Sons, Stourbridge, 1878. H. 4½ in. (11.4 cm.). Dema Glass Ltd.

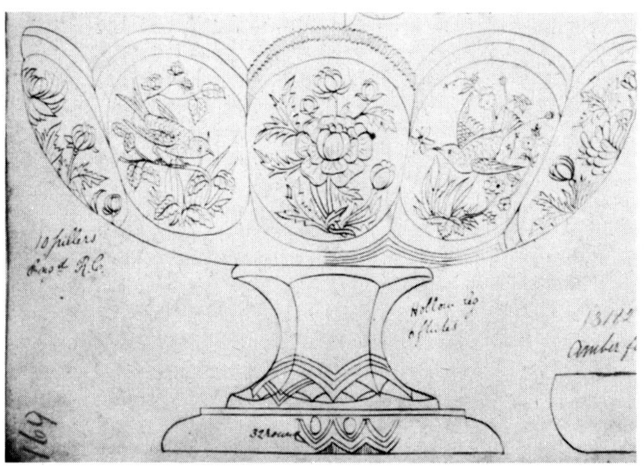

Figure 5. Drawing for bowl, rock crystal engraved. Thomas Webb and Sons, Stourbridge, pattern 13175, c. 1881-82. Dema Glass Ltd.

Figure 6. Drawing for wineglass, rock crystal engraved. Thomas Webb and Sons, Stourbridge, pattern 14276, 1883. Dema Glass Ltd.

Figure 7. Decanter, 'Hunting the Eagle', rock crystal engraved by F.E. Kny. Thomas Webb and Sons, Stourbridge, c. 1880. H. $14\frac{7}{8}$in. (37.8 cm.). Victoria and Albert Museum.

Figure 8. Champagne, rock crystal engraved. Stevens and Williams, Brierley Hill, 1879. H. $6\frac{1}{8}$in. (15.6 cm.). Royal Brierley Crystal.

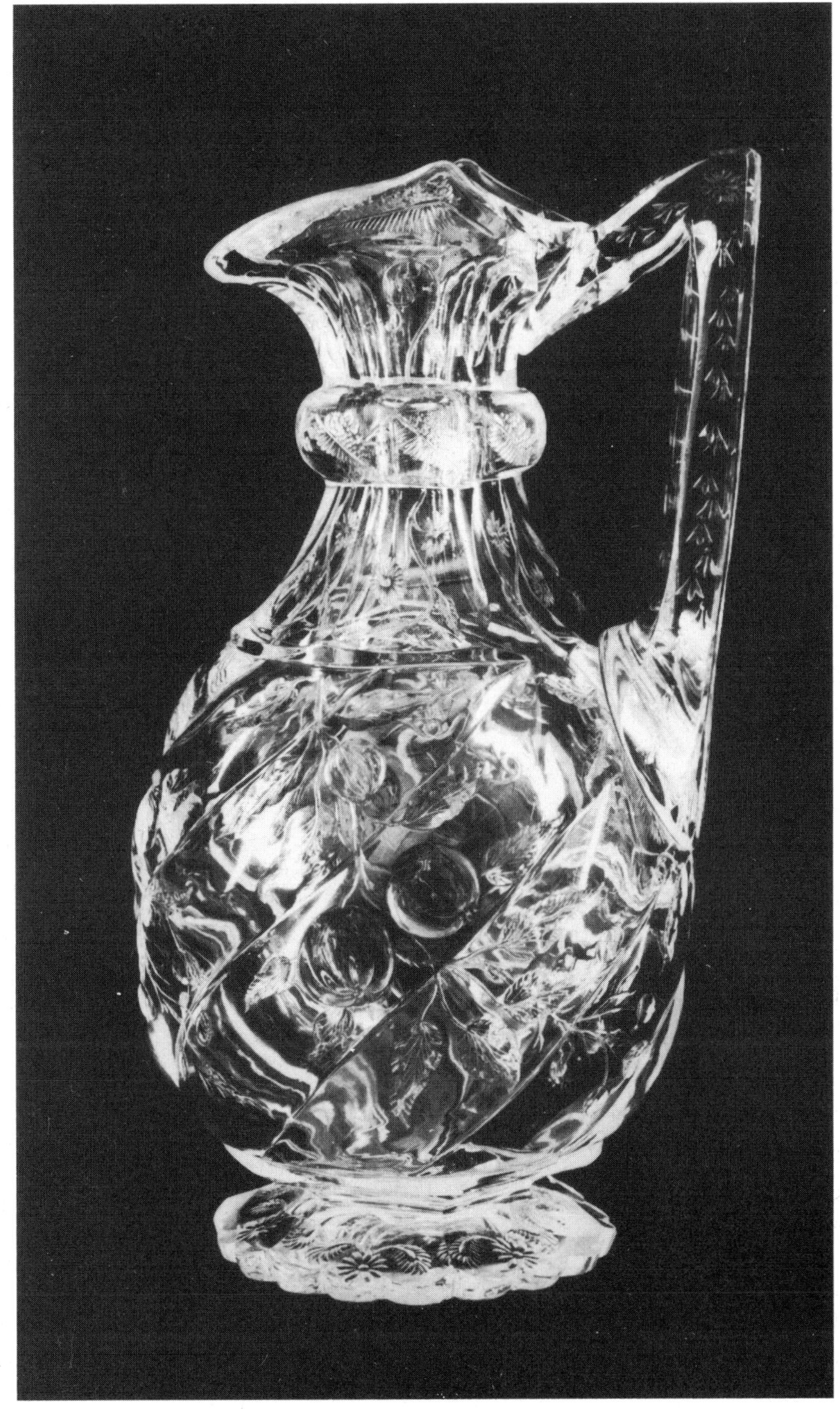

Figure 9. Jug, rock crystal engraved. Stevens and Williams, Brierley Hill, 1884. H. 8in. (20. 3 cm.). Royal Brierley Crystal.

Figure 10. Bowl, rock crystal engraved. Stevens and Williams, Brierley Hill, 1884. D. $10\frac{5}{8}$in. (26.9 cm.). Victoria and Albert Museum.

Figure 11. Drawing for wine, rock crystal engraved. Thomas Webb and Sons, Stourbridge, pattern 14660, 1884. Dema Glass Ltd.

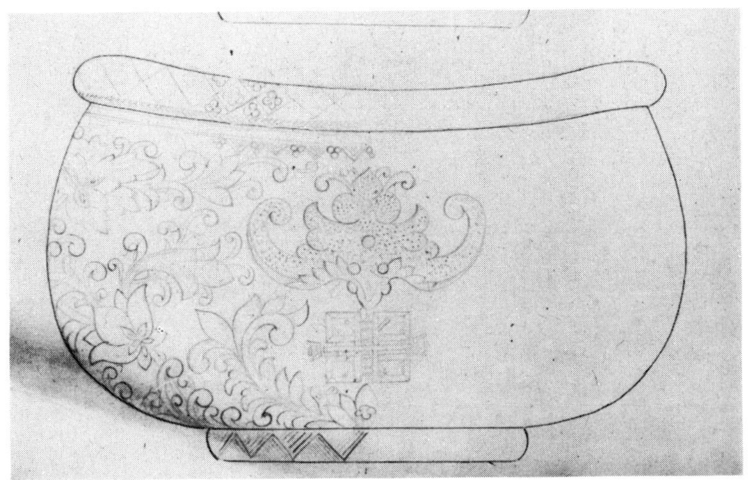

Figure 12. Drawing for bowl, rock crystal engraved. Thomas Webb and Sons, Stourbridge, pattern 14072, 1883. Dema Glass Ltd. (A bowl with closely similar design is in the Pilkington Glass Museum, St. Helens, no. 1967. 7).

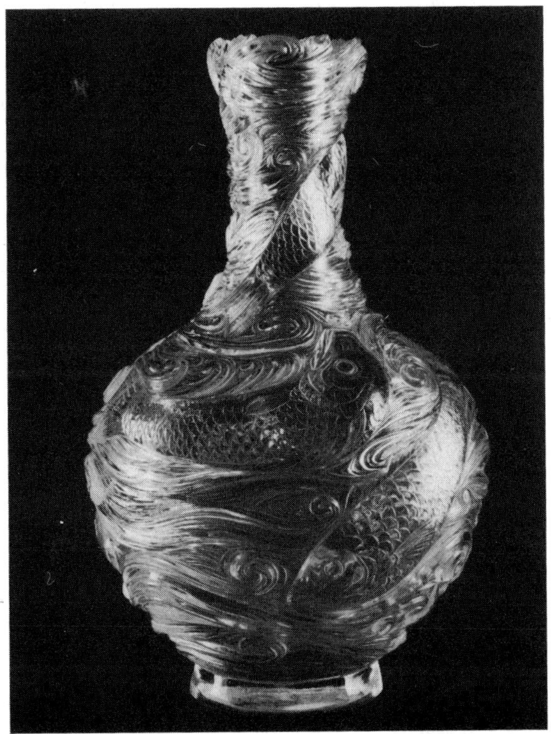

Figure 13. Vase, rock crystal engraved. Thomas Webb and Sons, Stourbridge, 1889. H. 12in. (30. 5 cm.). Private Collection.

Figure 14. Ewer, rock crystal engraved by William Fritsche. Thomas Webb and Sons, Stourbridge, 1886. H. $15^{3}/_{16}$ in. (38.6 cm.). Corning Museum of Glass, New York.

Figure 15. Drawing for wineglass, rock crystal engraved by William Fritsche. Thomas Webb and Sons, Stourbridge, pattern 13380, c. 1882. Dema Glass Ltd.

Figure 16. Drawing for bowl, rock crystal engraved by F. Kretschmann. Thomas Webb and Sons, Stourbridge, pattern 17457, 1889. Dema Glass Ltd.

Figure 17. Claret decanter, rock crystal engraved by William Fritsche. Thomas Webb and Sons, Stourbridge, 1897. H. $13^7/_8$in. (35. 3 cm.). Dudley Metropolitan Borough.

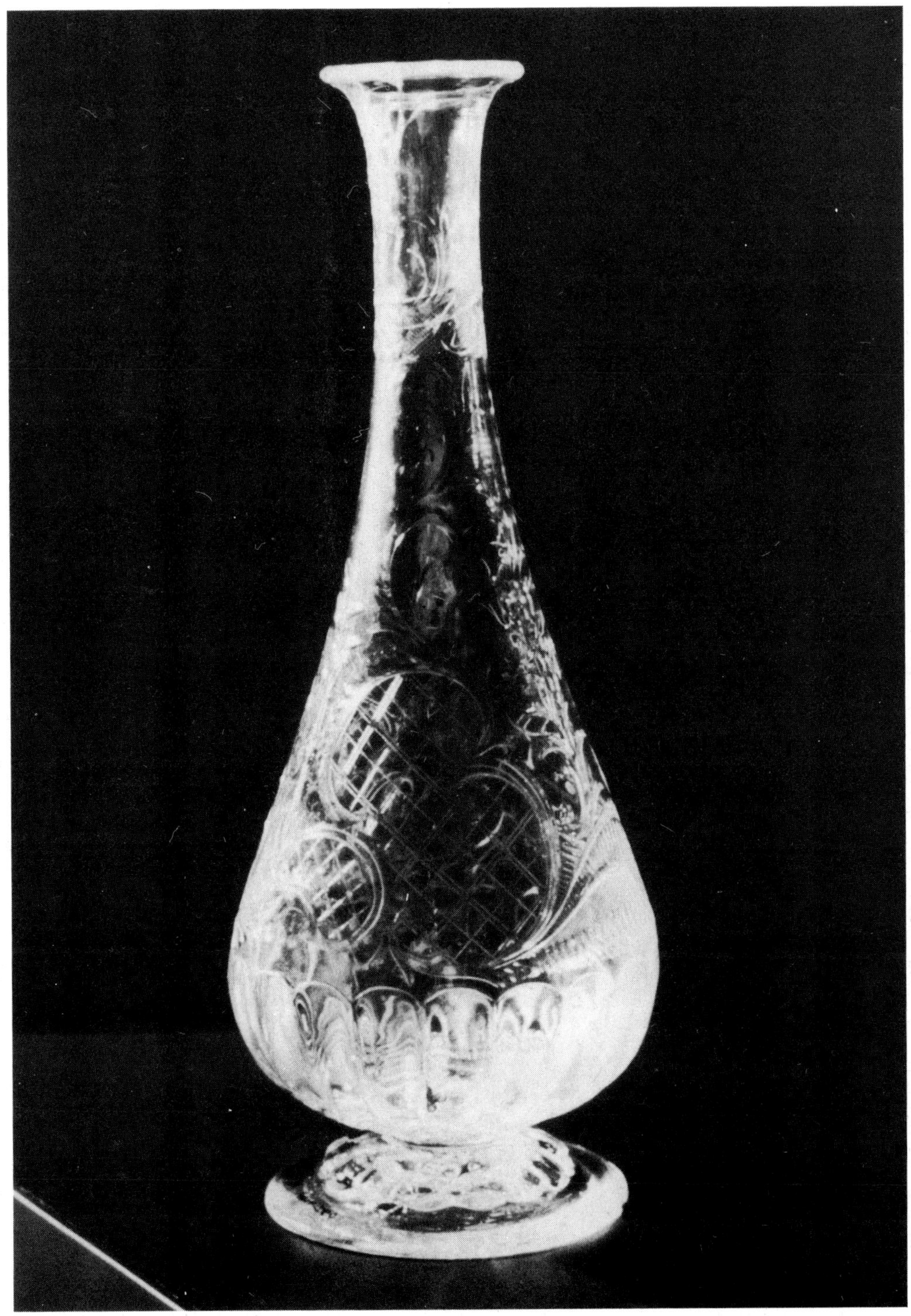

Figure 18. Decanter, rock crystal engraved. Thomas Webb and Sons, Stourbridge, 1894. H. 11½in. (29. 2 cm.). Merseyside County Museums.

Figure 19. Wineglass, rock crystal engraved by William Fritsche. Thomas Webb and Sons, Stourbridge, 1894. H. 4½in. (11.4 cm.). Dema Glass Ltd.

Figure 20. Wineglass, polished and matt engraved. Thomas Webb and Sons, Stourbridge, c. 1912. H. 4¾ in. (12.1 cm.). Dudley Metropolitan Borough.

Figure 21. Puff box, rock crystal engraved. Stevens and Williams, Brierley Hill, 1900. H. 3in. (7. 6 cm.), without cover. Victoria and Albert Museum.

Figure 22. Inkwell, rock crystal engraved. Stevens and Williams, Brierley Hill, 1902. H. 3in. (7. 6 cm.). Royal Brierley Crystal.

Figure 24. Tumbler, rock crystal engraved. Stevens and Williams, Brierley Hill, 1901. H. 4¼in. (10.8 cm.). Royal Brierley Crystal.

Figure 23. Decanter, rock crystal engraved. Stevens and Williams, Brierley Hill, 1903. H. 15½in. (39.4 cm.). Private Collection.

Reverse Painting on Glass

By RUDY ESWARIN

A Paper read to the Circle on 14 June, 1977.

My subject is painting on glass, in fact behind it, on the wrong side of the picture, as it were, and reversed in several other ways as well. Only recently has the awareness of this craft become more common among glass collectors. In the absence, however, of readily available specimens for examination outside selected museums and private collections, the interest remains regionally specialized. Since the more frequently encountered objects happen to be pictorial renderings on flat surfaces for use as wall decorations, it has been argued that this kind of painting has very little to do with glass, except in a mechanical way, and that it is seen and handled like any other picture under a sheet of glass in a frame. This is not so, as I shall try to demonstrate. Even though most of the reverse paintings coming on the market are of late date, collected by individuals and museums chiefly as expressions of folk art, this technique and its many uses belong to the art and history of glass.

Cold painting on glass (as opposed to fired enamelling), whichever side it is on, has been one of the ways to embellish a plain surface since late Antiquity. Once this surface has been covered with pigment, however, the opacity of the painting tends to diminish the importance of the glass, unless the item is a hollow vessel. One traditionally expects glass to be translucent, a see-through thing as opposed to a look-at thing, yet many chemical compositions and appearances of glass objects argue against this. Reverse painting as a type of glass decoration depends for its effect entirely on this very transparence of the material to which the opaque pigment is applied. The peculiarly unchanging freshness and the brilliance of the colour are uniquely partial to this process in which glass becomes an integral part of the painting in a way that is totally different from any other technique. We are looking at the picture through its *base*. The transparent support is simultaneously a fused cover of the artwork and, once broken, cannot be repaired more successfully than any other glass object.

In the production the normal process of painting is reversed. The artist *begins* with the highlights and the final detail of the image, progressing by moving backwards in successive layers of development until the all-covering last step, the background, has been reached. The word has lost here the technical connotation it has in other types of painting and describes only a visual effect. Under these conditions it follows that each brushstroke must sit just right, and each colour must blend properly. Second thoughts are not permitted, and corrections by overpainting are impossible without destroying the preceding work. When the panel is turned for viewing from the proper side, another reverse occurs as the elements on the left and the right of the picture are transposed; a particularly important factor when lettering is involved. The technique is rather demanding on the ability of the artist who is creating an original and must visualize the finished work in every detail before he touches the support surface with his brush. On the other hand, life can be much easier for the less competent. The mechanics of this process permit the development of simple routines and repetitive mass production patterns for anybody with a minimum of ability to follow quite successfully, as much of the available evidence amply demonstrates. The core of my presentation, by necessity, must be the considerable reverse-painted glass output in Central Europe during the one hundred and fifty years between the middle of the 18th and almost the end of the 19th century. This time segment encompasses the sources of the rapidly diminishing supply to the interested collector, and some well defined areas for research and study.

Cold painting on glass was known in various parts of the Roman world, and examples of polychrome images on the reverse surfaces of free-blown objects have survived. An important example, possibly from Antioch, Syria, about 200 A.D., is the well-known Paris Plate in the collection of the Corning Museum of Glass. The painting, depicting the mythological Judgement of Paris, is rendered in shades of gray, yellow, brown, violet, white and black, on a reddish background. The unfired pigment is applied to the convex underside of the plate, 21 cm in diameter, and the picture is viewed by looking into the shallow dish of colourless glass. A large group of painted vessels, some in poor condition, was found at Begram in Afghanistan. Of these, some were painted in cold colours with similar compositions, while others were enamelled.[1]

The decoration on the pyxis cover in the Newark Museum (fig. 1) has been applied the other way round. The figure of Eros, holding a bunch of grapes, is painted on the concave inside and seen through the outside surface when the cover is in place. Separated from the vessel, it belongs to a series of similar objects, and there are specimens in the Metropolitan Museum of Art, New

York, the British Museum and the Fitzwilliam Museum at Cambridge. They are in nearly every instance from Cyprus if the find spot is recorded.[2]

Numerous reverse-painted fragments exist, but complete objects in good condition are very rare. Most specimens appear to have originated in the Eastern Mediterranean area between the 1st and 3rd century A.D., and a vessel with cold-painted decoration cannot be found again until the 16th century. The chromatic surface techniques seem to have been forgotten during the interval, and the attempts to bridge a gap of some twelve centuries have not succeeded, leaving the sudden flowering of painting on flat glass in Northern Italy without apparent ancestry. I would like to venture the opinion that we have before us two separate developments of a basic idea—one belongs to Antiquity, the other to the Renaissance; both are different in concept as well as execution, and there is no continuity to look for.

By the 14th century unfired pigment was used on small glass panels with gold foil engravings as a filler and background colour to offset the metallic designs in the manner of the *fondi d'oro*. These panels were the inlaid decoration of reliquaries, crosses and house altars. In 1309 an order was issued in Paris making it illegal to apply gold or pigment to glass in imitation of enamel.[3] It had not occurred to anyone that coloured pigment could be used to create a work of art in its own right.

One of the earliest reverse-painted specimens with a truly polychrome pictorial rendering, in addition to the still dominant gold foil engraving, is a small oval panel in Turin. Of French origin from about 1420, and designed in the Gothic tradition of Cologne, the painting shows the Virgin and Child in green and red garments before a gilt arras, with an angel in white playing a harp. The Museo Civico di Torino has on permanent display one of the most comprehensive collections of panels and objects, beginning with the 14th and continuing into the 18th century. Venice and Padua were the leading early production centres, but a number of items have been made outside Italy in the Low Countries, France and Spain.

From the 15th century onward most of the subjects were derived from contemporary woodcuts and engravings after paintings by well-known artists in addition to original blocks cut for the purpose of producing prints. The 16th century panel depicting Christ under the Cross on his way to Calvary (fig. 3) appears to have been inspired by Martin Schongauer's engraving of the same subject, a popular model for a number of interpretations. The colours are mostly opaque tans and browns with a terracotta city in the mountains under a blue sky. The massive gold leaf areas are outlined by the Cross and the flying banner. The garments of the soldiers are rendered partly in translucent colours underlaid with gold to enrich the texture.

A similar effect was occasionally achieved by placing silver foil under transparent sienna paint shaded to simulate gold. The metallic surface helped to heighten the colour as can be seen on the Elizabethan English armorial panel, with the arms of Shuckburgh and Skeffington, in the glass collection of the Victoria and Albert Museum. A reverse painting based on a 16th century engraving by Marcantonio Raimondi after Mantegna can be seen in the same collection, together with other representative examples of the period.

During the 16th century much use was made of gold leaf under clear glass, or translucent pigment, in every reverse painting almost without exception. The refractive properties of the irregular glass surface and the freedom from oxidation and discolouration of the metal created an effect which could not be achieved with any other material or technique. The ambition of the artist was limited only by the available size of the glass, which was of such importance that it appeared preferable to make additions to the engraving, used as the pattern, rather than cut the panel down to the required dimensions. Two reverse paintings exist of the *Adoration* by Albrecht Dürer, one at the Veste Coburg, the other in the Bavarian National Museum, possibly by the same Venetian hand, where neutral pictorial elements have been added to stretch the image so that it would fill the available space on the almost square panel. In some instances artistic license was also taken to fit the model to the ability of the interpreter, but mostly the monochrome prints were quite agreeably transformed into sparkling paintings by craftsmen working in the centres of art and commerce north and south of the Alps. In Venice large circular dishes of clear glass and bowls with elaborate *lattimo* cane twists were further embellished by a colourful painting on the plain base, often of a female head after a contemporary woodcut. Examples can be found in a number of museums, and there are two splendid bowls in Turin.

By the early 17th century, tastes and fashions were beginning to change, and the reverse-painted glass production followed the trends. The stylistic and conceptual attitudes of high art were adopted, the forms became more supple, the colours shaded to create an illusion of depth, and the painting was executed with meticulous attention to realistic detail. Some technical achievements were truly spectacular, and one of the outstanding performers was Hans Jakob Sprüngli. Born in Zürich about 1559, he became known beyond the borders of his country and collaborated with top goldsmiths of the period in the production of work destined for the regal treasure vaults of Europe. We shall look at one example—the *Prunkhumpen* in the Swiss National Museum (fig. 2). Produced about 1620-1630, the silver-gilt mount of the tankard was made by the goldsmith Hans Heinrich Riva of Zürich, and the three reverse-painted polychrome panels on the outside are allegorical interpretations of Faith, Love and Hope by Sprüngli. The cylindrical interior glass liner is decorated along the circumference with a continuous procession of children in warlike costume, rendered in black on a gold background. The tankard is one of five objects in the Museum with paintings by Sprüngli, who must be seen as the most important and accomplished practitioner of this craft regardless of time and place.[4]

In the collection of Schloss Pommersfelden, near Coburg, there is a picture to epitomise the stylistic treatment of reverse paintings at the time leading into the 18th century. The picture of *Venus and Mars* is South German, about 1700, but painted in the Italianate manner after an original influenced by the Venetians of the late 16th century. It is a very handsome example of a style and purpose which would be served today by the so-called full colour reproduction. From here on, the gradual development of new ideas in the arts and sciences of the period, with their chief creative sources in France, Germany and England, changed the popular designs from the baroque to the rococo interpretation.

To simplify matters I would like to take a short cut to Augsburg which is one of the wellsprings in the development of reverse glass paintings from the high style of the city studio *Stilkunst* to what is now commonly accepted as folk art produced by cottage industry in widely dispersed country workshops. The situation in Augsburg around the turn of the century has been well documented by Dr. Gislind Ritz in her book *Hinterglasmalerei*.[5] The accomplished individuals working on glass, a Jan van Heyden (1637-1712) for instance, were seen as equals to a master painter. The lesser talents, however, belonged to the class of craftsmen and a slightly lower social order. As such they wished to benefit from the organized protection of a guild, and in 1693 the glass artists of Augsburg applied in a unique move for permission to join forces with other painters, sculptors, glaziers and makers of gold and silver wire. This led of course to the establishment of cooperative shops and the production of multiples, a logical and profitable move in a major centre of the graphic arts and printing. The multiples, in contrast to the later quantity output, retained some of the studio quality, and the repeats had an individual touch. A good example of the typical style around 1750 is the small painting of St. Bartholomew (fig. 10). It was quite common for many pictorial ideas to be treated as pairs—the *Good Shepherd* and the *Good Shepherdess* in flamboyant contemporary dress—or to be worked up in sets like the *Seasons* or the *Continents*, with symbolic imagery and attributes of a somewhat wild character.

The paintings in the Augsburg style (many originated in France) were sold far and wide during the second half of the 18th century, and the demand permitted the development of production in other localities influenced, but not controlled, by the main centre. In Oberammergau and the Staffelsee region south of Augsburg, particularly in Murnau on the old trade route to Italy, the city tradition was soon modified under the guidance of talented individuals, and a local style evolved, with a hint of the folk art to come. The Gege family workshop was prominent through several generations well into the 19th century, and the name is highly regarded by collectors. Some of the painters became known by name in almost every production area, but the vast majority worked in anonymous groups turning out incredible numbers of pictures on a great variety of subjects. It has been calculated that in the village of Raimundsreut, near the Bohemian border, from 30, 000 to 40, 000 reverse paintings were produced by five workmen in 1830. Between 1852 and 1864 the output of a single family workshop in Sandl was 386, 000 pictures, and other workers painted up to 200 a day.[6] It stands to reason that streamlined production methods were necessary to make this possible, and a system not unlike the modern assembly line concept was used in many locations.

As in any other mass production, a model to work from was a basic requirement. An engraving after Lukas Cranach, or a nameless popular print from Augsburg, was translated into a line drawing which became the indispensable outline pattern (Riss) to be laid under a precut sheet of cheap flat glass. The outline was redrawn on the surface following the pattern underneath the panel, and evidence seems to exist that the task was subsequently handled by several workers taking turns to apply the various colours until the painting was completed. Some of the colour areas were marked by numbers on the outline pattern.

The finished picture, a very popular Nativity from Sandl (fig. 4) can be compared with the pattern (fig. 5) from which the painting was made.

The design elements were transposed from left to right in the process of redrawing the outline. The basic colours are from the typical Sandl chromatic range: a warm, but bright red on the stable roof and on the garments, intermixed with similarly bright green and blue, against a mustard yellow background. The pattern was discovered rotting in a damp attic in the village and is now preserved, with about one hundred others from the same find, in the Museum für Volkskunde in Vienna.

In the workshop, having gone through the necessary number of steps to completion, the painted glass was fitted into a prefabricated simple softwood frame, usually of fir, with a shingle backing for protection, and stacked to be picked up by the distributor. In a cradle, designed for the purpose, a pedlar carried the stack of pictures on his back over hill and dale to farmhouses and distant markets, crossing a few borders on his way. A lithograph of a *Market Fair* in Transylvania, published in 1819 by F. Neuhauser, shows a salesman holding up a pole with crossbars, hung with pictures for the customers to see. This appears to be the stand of a single traveller who, having sold his portable stock, would return to the source.

The supply was geared to the demand, and the salesmen could order pictures for specific religious festivals and places of pilgrimage. The more popular images were available in one form or another from every workshop, and even special orders were accommodated to please a customer. The big business, however, was handled by distributing companies regularly shipping considerable quantities of paintings to representatives within the country and abroad from Hungary to Spain. A warehouse was established in Cádiz for handling shipments to the Americas, with a steady supply coming from the production centres in Bavaria and the Bohemian region, also the Black Forest and Alsace. The picture industry flourished in the geographical areas of Europe with a particularly strong Catholic orientation, and a population conditioned to visual representation of its religion. Every farmhouse had the best corner in the common room devoted to a display of the crucifix surrounded by pictures in brilliant colours, featuring the appropriate name-saints and protectors of the household, with periodic additions from the passing pedlar's cart as the family increased. The organized production methods and the massive output made it possible for these pictures to become truly a folk art within reach of the slender purses of the people.

The technology being essentially the same, and the subject matter similarly derived from common sources, the identification of specimens rests on stylistic differences particular to a production area or some specific locality. The basic styling of reverse glass paintings in the 19th century was shaped by two major factors. Like two confluent rivers joining to become a single stream, the one tributary originated in the painterly pictorial tradition of Augsburg, the other in the Bohemian glass industry and its predominantly mechanical methods of glass decoration (e.g. wheel-cutting and engraving). Although this attempt to build a theory on circumstantial evidence may oversimplify the situation, it helps to understand and recognize the formative influences.

The development of these pictures, rooted in a glassmaking tradition, cannot be traced to one dominant source, and we have to deal with a series of neighbourhoods in Silesia and Bohemia. A natural relationship exists between the southwestern region and the adjoining parts of Bavaria. Some centres, with a substantial output of reverse paintings identified by the names of specific villages, almost dovetail geographically, and it is not always a simple matter to make attributions on stylistic grounds. For instance, Buchers and Sandl are less than four miles apart, but an individual character has been ascribed to both in defiance of the proven interchange of workers and the probable use of the same outline patterns.[7]

Further north, on both sides of the wooded Riesengebirge mountain range, most of the individual glasshouses were surrounded by abundant supply of the all-important fuel for the furnaces. Among a number of centres Hirschberg, Warmbrunn and Haida are some of the more familiar names representing the popular concept of Bohemian glass. The relationship between hollow and flat glass is very close if we remember that the early small panes were made with the blowpipe by the crown or muff process. 'Venetian' mirrors were produced in Silesia by 1700, and glass frames were made later, with similar appearance and construction, to hold coloured prints of engravings. The decorative techniques to embellish the flat surfaces entailed cutting, wheel engraving, acid etching after Heinrich Schwanhardt's discovery about 1670, and toward the approaching end of the period came imitation of the aforementioned effects with common white paint. Coloured pigment was used in the tradition of enamelled hollow glass, and backed with a reflecting mercury coating. At some point it occurred to somebody to do the whole thing and paint a picture within the frame.

Of course, the various methods of glass decoration required special skills, and trained craftsmen were employed to work on different effects. In good time a stable relationship of long standing was created. When the glasshouse found itself sitting in a large clearing, with the cheap fuel used up, it had to move to a new place and a new forest, but workers who had established themselves in dwellings with small land holdings were unable or unwilling to follow. For these people it was a natural choice to settle for scanty income to continue the familiar work as individual suppliers. In due course a market opened for reverse paintings, and a cottage industry came into being at a number of locations near glasshouses. A foreman guided the activities of the workshop, maintained contact with sources of raw materials, often the former employer, and arranged distribution of the finished product. With this background information in mind, we can better appreciate the mirror picture (fig. 6) from South Bohemia, or possibly Raimundsreut, about 1800. It contains every type of the mechanical decoration under discussion as well as painted flowers around a polychrome central figure of the crucified Jesus. The ornamental framework consists of copper wheel abrasion combined with acid-etched flat areas and interspersed with cut and parcel-polished ovals. The legend below has been lettered with white paint. The background is completely mirrored, with large areas now blind, but with the oval printies still sparkling. A similar treatment can be seen in other specimens on a black background with the cut and abraded parts underlaid with gold which, together with a bright vermilion red and a cobalt blue pigment, creates a magnificent effect.

The trained craftsmen gradually disappeared, and the obsolete engraving wheel was replaced with a paintbrush. The picture of the *Infant Jesus with the Orb* (fig. 7), from Silesia north of the Riesengebirge mountains, illustrates the absence of mechanical means and the attempt to maintain the concept with a rendering in line and coloured pigment. The rosettes recall the star cut on the bottom of a tumbler, and the ornamental flowers in the upper corners can be found on enamelled glass vessels of the period. The placement and treatment of the figure reminds one of portrait engravings on the better spa glasses.

Once the special skills of a glass engraver were no longer available or desired, and everybody could simulate most design effects by other means, similar concepts and technology became quickly adopted throughout the producing areas. It is interesting to compare the pictorial and decorative treatment of a late painting from Raimundsreut (fig. 8) with one of about the same period from Alsace, possibly Colmar (fig. 9). They are distinctly and identifiably different in colour and layout, with a clearly established provenance from two areas 300 miles apart in a straight line and at least twice that by road. The obvious relationship, however, can be accepted as proof that the studio and the glasshouse traditions were ultimately combined in the reverse-painted pictures of the mid 19th century regardless of their geographical origin.

In the countries outside the arbitrary boundaries of 'Central Europe' this form of folk art was originally introduced by traders extending their territories as far as they could manage. In some areas the foreign inspiration was taken up and the ideas transformed according to long-established attitudes of the ethnic environment. The imported pictures acted as a catalyst rather than as examples to be followed by imitation.

It is now held that the Bohemian export of reverse paintings introduced the concept to Romania, where it was quickly modified and endowed with indigenous features thereby creating a virtually original style. The composition, for instance, and the unerring instinct for sparingly chosen colours give the Romanian icons, as they have rightly been called, an unmistakable character of their own, with the imagery strongly influenced by the Orthodox Eastern Church.

The production in Italy flourished in the South, particularly Sicily, where other colourful forms of folk art, like the painted carts and implements, provided a natural context. And yet, the influence of high art can be felt in some instances where the foreshortened figural composition seems to betray the attention the painter might have paid to the frescoes in his church. The Italian style seems to be the least affected by formal repeat patterns, and the painting has been done with an exuberantly baroque freedom of individual expression.

Spain, with its folk art tradition in painted ceramics and other ornamental crafts, was a receptive ground for inspiration derived from the Central European supply through the warehouses established in Cádiz since about 1750. Most of the production seems to have originated in the southern region of Andalusia, with some activity in the areas of Barcelona and Toledo. The Spanish pictures were once again interpretations rather than imitations, with the religious subjects often treated in a high-spirited secular manner in the styles and colours one expects to find in the South of Spain. The village belle appears to have been the model for the *divina pastora,* and a sweetly relaxed attitude seems to contradict the suffering of the Saviour.

Even outside Europe the exported ideas and

examples were helping to establish indigenous production of reverse-painted pictures as far away as the Orient. Persia and India must be mentioned because the growing popularity of the relatively late paintings has made specimens easily available to the collector, possibly produced to recent orders. The trade and missionary contacts of the 18th century introduced the concept to the Far East, and the resulting Chinese output returned to fill the better houses in Western Europe with reverse-painted mirrors set in Dutch cabinets and English Chippendale frames. Production was geared to export on all levels, and in the early 19th century sailors arrived back home with souvenir pictures featuring stereotyped geishas or loving couples in compromising situations.

A closer examination of the reverse paintings from international production areas or single locations spottily dispersed throughout the world, including North America, is beyond the scope of this paper. It will be necessary, however, to briefly mention two other methods of putting images on the reverse side of a glass panel—the foil engraving and the mezzotint transfer.

The similarity between painting with cold pigment and engraving metallic foil on the reverse side of a suitable transparent support must be perceived as the same relationship in which easel painting is paired with linear drawing. Both are technically different but thematically identical means of rendering a chosen image. Nowhere approaching glass paintings in popularity and variety, the foil engravings, sometimes called 'gold glass', appear in the late Roman period in the peculiar form of the *fondi d'oro* found imbedded as grave markers in the plaster walls of the Christian catacombs. Believed to be the bottoms of broken drinking vessels they are decorated with expertly engraved portraits to identify the burial site of a specific person, often with the addition of a written sentiment praising the good life. Also, the stylised figures of the more popular saints appear frequently, with pictorial references from the scriptures in renderings bearing the hallmarks of a stock selection prepared to order. This argues against the theory of the glass bottoms, in spite of the bowl fragments with similar decoration in the British Museum. The weight and construction of the gold glass medallions makes it difficult to imagine a drinking vessel with such a base, and not one complete object has been discovered. A few specimens can be found in the major museums, and the world's largest collection of well over a hundred is in the Museo Sacro of the Vatican Library, including some examples linked with the Jewish faith.

This type of glass decoration disappeared, along with the reverse-painted variety, and was not encountered again until the 13th century. Most of the engravings from the Renaissance have been attributed to centres in Northern Italy, notably Padua, where toward the end of the 14th century an account of working on gold foil appears in the famous manuscript *Il Libro dell'arte* by Cennino Cennini. Some exquisite small panels from that period can be seen in the Victoria and Albert Museum.

Reverse foil engraving on glass is widely known by the name *verre églomisé*. The origin of this unfortunate common label is best explained by quoting in full a paragraph from an article written for *The Connoisseur* by W. B. Honey.[8]

> 'A word is perhaps called for in explanation of the term 'Verre églomisé', which has for long been applied to this work, in common with the art of painting under glass. The name, as Mr. F. Sydney Eden rightly stated in *The Connoisseur* (June, 1932) is derived from that of one Glomy, an eighteenth century dealer. But the manner in which the name came to be adopted is not generally known. Glomy was also a picture framer, who introduced a fashion of surrounding a subject with a border of gilding and colour painted behind the glass, and prints framed in this way, when the style was taken up by others, were referred to in the trade as *églomisées*. The word was first adopted officially, so to speak, in a catalogue of the Musée de Cluny in 1852; when taken over by the Italians as *agglomizzato* it began to assume an air of respectable antiquity and became the customary term for all sorts of painting and gilding behind glass, of any date. Purists have denounced the term as an anachronism, as indeed it usually is, but in the absence of any other short name it is quite likely to survive.'

In the early 18th century reverse foil engraving was successfully established in certain areas, and craftsmen in the Low Countries, France and Bohemia employed this very suitable technique to decorate small objects from caskets to snuff boxes and jewellery. Wall pictures were the domain of more accomplished artists working after copperplate prints by the prolific engravers of the time, with city views and landscapes as particularly popular subjects.

A considerable technical ability is required to overcome the inherent difficulties of the process. As with reverse painting, no corrections can be made on the delicate engraving. The opaque properties of the material do not permit a pattern to be laid under the glass, and the work area looks like a metal plate on the surface of which the image is drawn with the sharp point of a needle. After the completion of the drawing the panel is covered with a layer of paint for contrast and protection. This coating is seen from the other side behind the linework of the engraving, and the effect is not unlike that of a print on a gold background.

The best known practitioner of this art form was Jonas Zeuner (1727-1814) of Amsterdam. His work is well represented in major collections, and a splendid panel depicting the Sadler's Wells Theatre is on display in the glass department of the Victoria and Albert Museum. Zeuner engraved a number of English views, but it is not certain that he ever actually worked in England. A characteristic example of his style is provided by a riverside village scene in the Corning Museum of Glass (fig. 11). The landscape has been treated like a metallic cutout in front of a sky rendered in soft tones of pinkish gray colours, with cloud formations and birds in flight. This treatment of the sky as a device to quickly fill a large area of the panel, and the very effective use of silver foil in combination with two shades of gold to make up the engraved area have become a Zeuner trademark. The modern category of mixed media would perfectly fit his standard choice of materials and layouts.

As in the case of studio painting, the foil engraving technique also found its way into folk art, and the early 19th century craftsmen in Silesia and Bohemia produced signed panels with engravings in silver or gold foil featuring religious and secular subjects.

No illustrations of the so-called English Glass Pictures are needed for members of the Glass Circle, and I shall touch only briefly on this third type of reverse-painted glass. In 1959 Jeffrey Rose read a paper to the Circle on *The English Glass Pictures or the Art of Painting Mezzotinto,* and there is very little that can be added to his thorough coverage of the subject, even after nearly twenty years of further study.

During the 18th century, and up to the Victorian period, these pictures were a natural part of the decorative components in a household of refinement. The apparently insatiable appetite of the Georgians for portraits depicting persons of quality was met by royalty and nobility at one end of the scale, actresses and ladies of fashion at the other. Paintings by Sir Godfrey Kneller and other popular portrait artists of the time were made into mezzotints, and the soft velvety tones of the print were particularly suitable for colouring behind glass. It has been said that the mezzotint transfers were put together, or at least finished, by ladies of leisure as a hobby, and how-to-do-it instructions were indeed printed in contemporary manuals. Although the development might have been started by individuals, commercial production soon took over.

The effective and relatively cheap pictures could be manufactured quickly in a large selection. They were widely distributed and even exported to the Colonies. Advertisements appeared in the *Boston Gazette* and other newspapers for mezzo-transfers, featuring as subjects: the *Months,* the *Seasons,* the *Four Times of Day,* the *Five Senses,* the *Elements,* the *Royal Family* and various prints after Hogarth and Reynolds. The *Four Seasons* after Rosalba were extremely popular, and complete sets keep turning up in the salerooms of London.

The production process consists of a few basically simple steps. First lay a moistened mezzotint on a tacky sheet of varnished glass, printed side down, and wait for the bond to set. Then thoroughly soften the paper with lots of water, and rub it off carefully in rolled little bits so that only the ink remains adhering to the glass. After drying, the image can be coloured in layers of transparent glazes until the desired effect has been achieved. Opaque white paint will provide the background cover and reflect the light to bring out the subtle colouring. Rough and messy at first, the process is very delicate in the finish, and at least some artistic talent may be required to do the job well.

The Victorians changed the popular taste and interrupted the continuity by putting the pictures away in attics and other depositories, from which they have been only recently retrieved, so that we must view the English glass pictures as a purely Georgian phenomenon. Modern attitudes have hardened against the whole concept of these pictures, and make it difficult for us to appreciate them for themselves. We tend to view them in an antiquarian spirit, as examples of an old craft.

Conversely, I would like to think that all is well with the art of reverse painting on glass, and that the concept did not do what it is supposed to have done—meekly give up the ghost sometime in the late 19th century. Although it ceased to play a significant economic role and was replaced by the atrocious oleo prints, the art form was carried over to the present time by some individuals continuing the tradition and by others who picked it up anew. In Sandl, for instance, some work was done in the old style beyond the turn of the century. Around 1910 Wassily Kandinsky, Gabriele Münter and a few others of the group of artists *Der Blaue Reiter* picked up the thread in Murnau and continued to experiment with the technique for their own purposes. In 1918 Picard published *Expressionistische Bauernmalerei*, the first book on the subject relating it to artistic attitudes. In Bern there is a collection of reverse paintings by Paul Klee, and serious contemporary work is being done in a number of places in Central Europe, notably around Munich.

Contrary to the widely accepted notion that the Blue Rider group must be credited with the 'discovery' of reverse painting as folk art worth preserving, it may be that their real contribution lies in the fact of their having done something new with it. By taking the well established technique away from utilitarian applications and placing it back in the realm of pure art, they closed the proverbial circle, but kept the options open.

One cannot help but wonder why anybody would willingly go through the misery of painting backwards on a piece of glass at a time when the most advanced techniques and materials are available for the asking. Perhaps one should look for the answer in the simple statement by the rather sophisticated 'naive' Yugoslavian painter Ivan Generalić:

> 'colours on glass are more beautiful, more luminous'.[9]

NOTES

1. The Corning Museum of Glass, *Glass from the Ancient World, The Ray Winfield Smith Collection,* Corning, New York (1957), p. 165.
2. The Corning Museum of Glass, *op. cit.*, p. 167.
3. Gislind M. Ritz, *Hinterglasmalerei,* Munich, Verlag Georg D. W. Callwey (1972), p. 8.
4. Admirably described by Franz-Adrian Dreier, 'Hans Jakob Sprüngli aus Zürich als Hinterglasmaler', *Zeitschrift für schweizerische Archäologie und Kunstgeschichte,* Band 21, Heft 1 (1961), pp. 5-18.
5. Gislind M. Ritz, *op. cit.*, p. 49.
6. Wolfgang Brückner, *Hinterglasmalerei* (Keysers Kunst- und Antiquitätenbuch, Band 3), Munich, Keysersche Verlagsbuchhandlung (1976), p. 89.
7. Leopold Schmidt, *Hinterglas*, Salzburg, Residenz Verlag, (1972), p. 34.
8. W. B. Honey, 'Gold-Engraving under Glass', *The Connoisseur,* 92 (December, 1933), pp. 372-375.
9. Nebojša Tomašević, *The Magic World of Ivan Generalić,* New York, Rizzoli International Publications Inc. (1976), p. 93.

Selected Bibliography

Herbert Wolfgang Keiser, *Die Deutsche Hinterglasmalerei,* Munich, F. Bruckmann Verlag (1937)

Cornel Irimie and Marcela Focsa, *Romanian Icons painted on Glass,* London, Thames and Hudson (1970)

Leon Kieffer, *La Peinture sous Verre en Alsace,* Strasbourg, Librairie Istra (1972)

Antonino Buttitta, *La Pittura su Vetro in Sicilia,* Palermo, Sellerio Editore (1972)

Friedrich Knaipp, *Hinterglasbilder,* Linz/Donau, Verlag J. Wimmer (1973)

Raimund Schuster, *Auf Glas Gemalt,* Regensburg, Verlag Friedrich Pustet (1973)

Max Seidel, *Hinterglasbilder,* Stuttgart, Belser Verlag (1978)

Figure 1. Pyxis lid, Roman (Cyprus), 2nd-3rd century A.D. D. $3\frac{3}{8}$in. (8. 5 cm.). The Newark Museum, New Jersey (73. 132).

Figure 2. Tankard, Swiss (Zürich), 1620-1630. H. $7\frac{5}{8}$in. (19. 5 cm.) Swiss National Museum, Zürich (32365).

Figure 3. *Christ bearing the Cross,* Italian (possibly Venice), 16th century. $9\frac{1}{8} \times 7\frac{5}{8}$in. (23 × 19.5 cm.). Private collection.

Figure 4. *Nativity*, Austrian (Sandl), ca. 1840. $9\frac{7}{8} \times 6\frac{5}{8}$in. (25 × 17 cm.). Private collection.

Figure 5. Outline pattern, Austrian (Sandl), ca. 1840 approx. $10\frac{1}{4} \times 7\frac{1}{8}$ in. (26×18 cm.). After an original in the Museum für Volkskunde, Vienna.

Figure 6. *Crucifixion,* Bohemian, ca. 1800. $10\frac{1}{4} \times 6\frac{7}{8}$in. (26.5 × 17.5 cm.). Private collection.

Figure 7. *Jesus with Orb,* Silesian, ca. 1820. $10^{3}/_{4} \times 6^{5}/_{8}$ in. (27.5 × 17 cm.). Private collection.

Figure 8. *Virgin and Child,* German (Raimundsreut), ca. 1860. $9\frac{7}{8} \times 6\frac{7}{8}$ in. (25 × 17.5 cm.). Private collection.

Figure 9. *St. John*, Alsatian (possibly Colmar), ca. 1860. $9\frac{1}{2} \times 6\frac{7}{8}$in. (24 × 17.5 cm.). Private collection.

Figure 10. *St. Bartholomew,* German (Augsburg), ca. 1750. $9\frac{7}{8} \times 7\frac{1}{2}$ in. (25 × 19 cm.). Private collection.

Figure 11. Landscape by Jonas Zeuner, The Netherlands (Amsterdam), ca. 1785. $9\frac{7}{8} \times 17$in. (25.9×43.2 cm.). The Corning Museum of Glass (53. 3. 32).

The Manchester Glass Industry

By ROGER DODSWORTH

A Paper read to the Circle on 18 March, 1980

Manchester glass is one of the least-known aspects of English Glass History. Being primarily a Victorian industry it has suffered the neglect common to most 19th century English glass. However, the principal reason why Manchester glass is so little known is simply that until quite recently most writers on glass seem to have been unaware that the town had ever possessed a glass industry. Even when the industry was at its height contemporaries had difficulty in connecting Manchester with glass. In 1851 one wrote: 'One is so apt to associate the manufacturing production of Manchester with cotton and calico as to feel some surprise to see an exhibition of beautiful glassware emanating from that busy town. . . . Moreover it is not generally known that not less than twenty-five tons of flint glass are at the present time produced weekly in Manchester where the establishment of Messrs. Molineaux and Webb takes the lead in this department of industrial art.'[1]

The Manchester Glass Industry was first put on the map by Hugh Wakefield in his pioneering work *19th century British Glass*, published in 1961. Before then the only writers to refer to Manchester had been Francis Buckley, who uncovered evidence of glassmaking in the town from his research into 18th and 19th century journals and newspapers[2], and Harry Powell[3] and Angus-Butterworth[4], both of whom had worked a lifetime in the industry and for that reason were aware of the part that Manchester had played. In the 1960's the Victoria and Albert Museum began to collect Manchester pressed glass for the now defunct and much-missed Circulation Department, and one or two pieces were included in the department's travelling exhibition on Victorian Glass. In the early 1970s the City Art Gallery, Manchester, also began collecting pressed glass, and some valuable research into the history of the industry was begun by Charles Hajdamach of the Art Gallery staff, which has continued in fits and starts since then. Considerable progress has been made in the last ten years particularly in the identification of the pressed glass. But the glass itself only tells part of the story and a complete picture of how the industry developed will be obtained only by laborious research into contemporary records such as Directories, maps, photographs, newspapers and insurance documents, none of which have been systematically investigated yet.

I intend to divide my talk into two parts. In the first I shall discuss the early history of glassmaking in Manchester and the cut and engraved glass of Molineaux Webb, and in the second part Manchester pressed glass, with special reference to the best-known producer, John Derbyshire.

Glassmaking in the Manchester area goes back at least as far as the early 17th century, when a glasshouse was established at Haughton Green, Denton, about five miles east of the city centre.[5] Glassmaking on the site ceased probably during the 1650s and there then ensued a long gap in activity until the mid 18th century, when there were one or two isolated, unsuccessful attempts to set up glasshouses, listed by Buckley. The pace quickens towards the end of the 18th century. Imison and King opened a works in Newton Heath, Manchester, in 1785 for the manufacture of all sorts of glass wares, and in 1795 the *Manchester Mercury* refers to the firm of Atherton and Whalley, cut and engraved glass manufacturers. Butterworth Bros. Ltd., the last Manchester firm to close, were said to have been the successors to a business started in Newton Heath as long ago as 1795.[6] Robert Charleston has discovered a reference to an engraver named Unsworth in Manchester around the turn of the century, and by 1821 the industry was well enough established for glassblowers to take part in the processions which marked the coronation of George IV. However, it is not until about 1830 that Manchester can begin to be called an important glassmaking centre.

At first the evidence is rather confused. For instance, the 1833 *Directories* list six glass firms, Joshua Bower & Co., John Haddock and Co., Joshua Henzell & Co., Molineaux Webb Ellis & Co., Robinson Perrin and Maginnis, and West and Bromilow. However, according to the Parliamentary Commission of Enquiry into the Excise Duty, which is probably more reliable, the manufacturers that year were Thomas Molineaux, William Robinson, William Maginnis & Co., Daniel Watson & Co. and Frederick Fareham. Whatever the answer may be, 'in 1833 Manchester appears rather suddenly and unexpectedly in the Parliamentary List as one of the more important glassmaking areas in England.'[7]

What caused the emergence of a glass industry in Manchester at this time? One incentive must have been the rapid growth in the population of the town, coupled with the absence of any existing glass industry to take advantage of this expanding market. Between 1801 and 1831 the population doubled from 70, 000 to 140, 000, having trebled in the previous thirty years, and from 1831 to 1851 it doubled again to 300, 000. Neighbouring towns such as Bolton, Bury, Oldham and Rochdale were also expanding fast.

The glass industry must also have been encouraged by the excellent communications system which the town enjoyed. The navigable waters of the Irwell and Mersey plus a whole network of canals and railways gave Manchester access not only to the rest of the country but also to the principal ports of Liverpool, London and Hull, from which 'articles made at its manufactories could be wafted to the most distant shores of both hemispheres', as a contemporary put it. The raw materials for glass could be imported via the same routes, though one material which Manchester had in abundance on its own doorstep was coal for firing the furnaces. The industry established itself in a district called Ancoats, about half a mile north-east of the town centre. In 1830 Ancoats was a newly built-up area on the edge of Manchester, adjoining open countryside. A canal with various branches ran through it, enabling materials to be brought right to the factory doors. The following description was recorded in 1844 and gives some idea of how the area may have looked. 'Manchester is certainly a strange place. Nothing is to be seen but houses blackened by smoke and in the external parts of the towns half empty dirty ditches between smoking factories of different kinds, all built with regard to practical utility and without any respect at all for external beauty . . . I could not help being forcibly struck by the peculiar dense atmosphere which hangs over these towns in which hundreds of chimneys are continually vomiting forth clouds of smoke. The light even is quite different from what it is elsewhere. What a curious red colour was presented by the evening light this evening. It is not like a mist nor like dust nor like smoke but is a sort of mixture of these three ingredients, condensed moreover by the particular chemical exhalations of such towns.'

Today all the smoke has gone and most of the industry. Ancoats is in fact a typical inner city area, a combination of decaying factories and new housing, at first tower blocks and now 'low-rise'. The Kirby Street site of Molineaux Webb has completely disappeared, but fortunately Jersey Street and Poland Street, the heart of the glass quarter, are still more or less intact, though it has not yet been established whether any of the buildings still standing were once glass factories.

The most important of all the Manchester factories was Molineaux, Webb & Co. The firm was founded in 1827 and until 1831 went under the name of Maginnis Molineaux & Co. Between 1832 and 1845 it traded as Molineaux Webb Ellis & Co., flint glass and vial manufacturers, and from 1845 until closure in 1931 as Molineaux Webb & Co. Both Maginnis and Molineaux are very shadowy figures. Maginnis appears to have left the firm about 1831 and set up a rival concern. When the Molineaux connection ceased we do not know but it was certainly by 1859, for nobody of that name is mentioned at the celebrations which marked the retirement of Thomas Webb II. However, the name Molineaux was retained in the firm's title until the end, possibly to avoid confusion with the Webb firms in Stourbridge.

The Webbs were a glassmaking family from Warrington. The first member of the family we know about is a Thomas Webb, glassmaker, who was born in 1753 and died in 1839. It was his son, Thomas Webb II, who was instrumental in founding Molineaux Webb in 1827. He was born in Warrington in 1797 and died in 1873. On his retirement in 1859 a great banquet was held at the works and he was presented with a testimonial which included an illuminated address inscribed:

> 'This vellum, as a record and memorial, with a Silver Tea and Coffee Service and Cigar Case were presented to Thomas Webb Esq by the Workpeople of the Manchester Flint Glass Works, on his retirement from that concern. He was one of the first founders of those Works thirty-three years ago and many of the subscribers to the Testimonials were servants under and co-workers with him from the beginning. As an earnest and sincere expression of regard, one more unaminous could not have been rendered; all in that establishment having cheerfully contributed in proportion to their means. Manchester Flint Glass Works, December 30th 1859.'[8]

After 1859 the firm was carried on by Thomas's son, Thomas George Webb (fig. 1), with a partner called David Wilkinson. It was under Thomas George's grandson, Duncan Webb II, that the factory closed in 1931.

We should know virtually nothing about Molineaux Webb's cut and engraved glass were it not for the existence of a magnificent factory pattern book which was sold by Duncan Webb II's daughter at Sotheby's Belgravia in 1977 and purchased by The City Art Gallery, Manchester. The book, which has 194 pages (14" × 10"), contains just over 2000 designs in pen and ink and occasionally colour wash, and is embellished throughout with numerous small decorative flourishes. Coloured and cased glass is illustrated besides crystal. Decoration is principally cut or engraved, though reference is made to etching and gilding and some patterns may have been enamelled. Pressed glass is not included. The book is arranged in sections according to type of object. The largest section is devoted to Decanters, which have over 500 designs, followed by sugar basins and creams, caraffes and tumblers, water jugs and goblets (figs. 2-3), and celeries. The more obscure branches of Victorian tableware, however, such as marmalades, mustards (fig. 4), radishes and knife rests only receive a page or two each.

The pattern book was compiled perhaps about 1870 from five separate pattern books, entitled The Old Vase Sketch Book, The Large Book, No. 1, No. 2 and No. 3 or the New Sketch Book. Each section contains designs from some or all of these books, and the transition from one to another is acknowledged with a note such as 'end of No. 2 Book. New Book commences'. The Old Vase Sketch Book is the earliest in date and shows the heavy, broad-fluted style of cutting that was so popular in this country from the 1820s to the 1840s. Some of the patterns have names such as 'William IV' and 'Reform' and they must date from the very first years of the firm's existence. The latest patterns are found in No. 3 or The New Book, which cannot date much before about 1870. The shapes of the water jugs and goblets in particular betray a strong classical or eastern influence, and several are decorated with the ubiquitous fern motif, which only became popular in the 1860s. No. 1 Book includes several pieces that Molineaux Webb exhibited at the Great Exhibition, which is the only occasion where a precise date can be given to any of the pattern numbers. Other examples of the firm's Great Exhibition glass, for which it was awarded a bronze medal, were illustrated in the 1851 *Art Journal* (fig. 5).[9] Ruby-cased glass featured prominently along with ordinary cut crystal, but the most interesting piece was an opalescent vase decorated with a classical scene from Flaxman showing Diomed casting his spear at Mars. According to the *Art Journal* the scene was engraved, but as the vase is opalescent it is more likely to have been transfer-printed from an engraved plate, a technique usually associated with Richardson's of Wordsley. Another interesting style made by Molineaux Webb around the time of the Great Exhibition was iced or crackle glass.

Two pieces of glass were sold with the pattern book, a heavily cut amber decanter (figs. 7-8) from the 1850s (pattern 7085) and a frosted comport with a ruby rim and an engraved band of ornament, c. 1865, and the pattern book may lead to the discovery of others in time. Duncan Webb's daughter has a number of glasses which family tradition says were made at Molineaux Webb but which, unfortunately, cannot be traced in the pattern book. These include a claret decanter and goblet, finely engraved with classical grotesque ornament (fig. 9), and a fascinating small tumbler engraved in Bohemian style with a woodland scene and signed 'A. Böhm.' August Böhm was one of the foremost Bohemian engravers of the 19th century. His masterpiece is undoubtedly the large vase and cover depicting the Battle of the River Granicus fought between Alexander The Great and King Darius in 334 B.C., which he executed at Meistersdorf in 1840 and which is mentioned by Apsley Pellatt in *Curiosities of Glassmaking*. Böhm is said to have worked in England, and it is fascinating to speculate that he may have been for a time in Manchester with Molineaux Webb. On balance, however, it is more likely that the tumbler is a Bohemian glass which Thomas Webb II somehow acquired.

One Bohemian who definitely did work in Manchester was Wilhelm Pohl, who was born in 1839 and came from a distinguished line of glass engravers. He is recorded first at Edinburgh and then in Warrington before arriving in Manchester in 1873, where he worked for the Prussia Street Flint Glass Works of Andrew Ker & Co.[10] His most important piece is the Manchester Town Hall Goblet (fig. 10) which was presented to the Mayor, Mr. Alderman Heywood, by the workmen of Messrs. Andrew Ker & Co. on the opening of the spectacular new Gothic Town Hall in 1877. It is engraved with a view of The Town Hall on one side and was apparently going to have a portrait of the Mayor on the other, but this was not carried out.[11] The goblet has had a chequered history. Following some correspondence in the local press in 1926, it came to light that the goblet was no longer in The Town Hall. In 1951 a newspaper article appeared on Pohl's daughter and the mystery of the missing goblet but once again no clue was found of its whereabouts. Finally in 1973 the Art Gallery in Manchester received a letter out of the blue from an Antique Dealer in Co. Durham saying that he had a goblet engraved with Manchester Town Hall and would the Gallery be interested in buying it, which eventually it did. Pohl's family in Manchester have other examples of his glass including two jugs engraved with an officer on horseback and The Devil's Glen, Co. Wicklow, and a rummer showing Woolf's house and St. Mary's, Sankey, near Warrington.

These glasses by Pohl, the Molineaux Webb decanter and comport sold with the pattern book, and the pieces belonging to the daughter of Duncan Webb, are almost the only known examples of cut and engraved glass made in Manchester. Other factories such as Percival Vickers, Burtles Tate & Co. (fig. 6), and the Derbyshire Bros. were also producing this type of work, but not a single example has been identified yet.

If Manchester glass is known at all, it is the pressed glass people have heard of. The frequent appearance of the diamond registry mark on pressed wares has enabled a number of pieces to be traced to particular Manchester factories, while one manufacturer, John Derbyshire, even employed a trade mark, for which collectors and historians will be eternally grateful. Where the glass itself does not survive, the drawings that accompany the registered designs provide invaluable information.

Pressed glass was being made in Manchester at least as early as 1848. This is the date of a most interesting letter written by Thomas Webb II to the Warrington firm of Robinson & Skinner, in which he describes how the manufacture of pressed glass is carried on at Molineaux Webb.[12] The men worked a basic sixty-six hour week made up of eleven moves or shifts of six hours each. They operated in teams of six called a 'place', which consisted of a presser, melter and gatherer, and three boys, the sticker-up, taker-in and warmer-in. The pressers received 21/- to 23/- a week before overtime, the melters 21/- to 24/-, and the gatherers 14/- to 16/-. The melter had the important job of taking the newly-pressed article to the furnace mouth and manipulating it in the heat to soften rough edges and seam marks but without destroying the sharpness and detail of the design. A contemporary writer, George Dodd,[13] mentions other difficulties in pressing glass. 'The process', he says, 'is said to be cheap and expeditious but to require much skill. If the quantity of glass be too large, the over-plus gives considerable trouble, if too little the article is spoiled. If the die and plunger be too hot, the glass will adhere to them, if too cold the surface of the glass becomes cloudy and imperfect.'

Returning to Thomas Webb's letter, the list of products includes tumblers, salts, sugar basins, dishes and plates, mustards, pickles and butters. Large dishes were the most difficult job. Only about eighty or a hundred could be made in six hours, whereas up to 500 half-pint tumblers could be produced in that time. Unfortunately no Molineaux Webb pressed glass can be identified until the 1860s, when the factory began regularly to register designs. Another firm early in the field of pressed glass was Percival Yates and Vickers of Jersey Street, Ancoats, founded in 1844, but once again no examples are known before the 1860s.

John Derbyshire of Salford is undoubtedly the best-known pressed glass manufacturer, thanks to his JD and anchor trade mark. The series of paperweights in animal and human forms which he produced in the 1870s are among the most original and attractive examples of pressed glass ever made in this country. The earliest reference to the glassmaking activities of the Derbyshire family comes in 1858, when James Derbyshire, John's elder brother, set up a factory known as the British Union Flint Glass Works at 248 City Road, Hulme. Hulme was the other glassmaking district of Manchester, situated about half a mile south of the town centre. By 1867 James had been joined by his two brothers, John and Thomas, and they established another factory called The Bridgwater Flint Glass Works in Trentham Street, Hulme. The brothers operated both works until 1873, when John left to start his own company at Regent Road, Salford, where he produced cut, engraved and etched glass as well as pressed. He is recorded there until 1876 and it was during those four years only that the JD and anchor trade mark was used. After 1876 mention of John Derybshire ceases and the Salford factory was renamed The Regent Flint Glass Co. Meanwhile James Derbyshire and Sons continued to run one if not both of the works in Hulme until 1881, when the firm is listed not only at City Road but also at Regent Road, Salford.

As only a handful of pieces from the Hulme factories have so far been found, we have to turn to the diamond-registered designs and the accompanying drawings for information on the early glass by the Derbyshires. The brothers appear to have concentrated on ordinary tableware such as ale glasses, goblets (fig. 15), sugar basins, dishes, celeries, and comports, decorated either in imitation of cut glass or with simplified engravers' patterns set against a contrasting frosted background. A particularly popular design with the Derbyshires but also with their rivals, Molineaux Webb, was the Greek Key and both firms registered at least two versions each in 1865. Later, Derbyshire's attempted some more ambitious pieces such as a dolphin comport and a Roman vase, registered in 1872.

While he did not neglect simple pressed tableware at Salford, the move there in 1873 enabled John Derbyshire to give more attention to decorative pressed glass than there had been at Hulme. The inspiration for several of the designs seems to have come from ceramics. The greyhound paperweight (registered September, 1874) owes an obvious debt to 19th century Staffordshire figures, while the figures of *Punch* and *Judy* are found in 19th century salt-glazed stoneware and also appear in metalwork. John Derbyshire did not register his *Punch* and *Judy* and this is puzzling.

Either he did not feel the designs needed protecting or for some technical reasons he was prohibited from doing so. Judging by the numbers that have survived and the range of colours used (blue, green, frosted and clear) John Derbyshire's most successful product must have been the lion paperweight (registered July, 1874) based on the lions by Landseer at the foot of Nelson's column (fig. 11). Derbyshire also produced a slightly smaller lion with front legs crossed (fig. 12), but why he chose to make two, which came first and why only one was registered, we do not know.

Another problem is raised by a full length figure of the young *Queen Victoria* (fig. 13). Although very similar in style to the *Britannia* paperweight which Derbyshire registered in November, 1874, it carries neither trade mark nor registry mark and therefore may possibly have been made by a rival Manchester firm. That there was close competition between the Manchester firms is shown by the episode of the sphinxes. In the early 1870s negotiations began concerning the possibility of moving the obelisk known as Cleopatra's needle from Egypt to London. This caught the public imagination and inspired Molineaux Webb in July, 1875, to register a paperweight in the form of a sphinx in black glass, derived from Wedgwood basalt ware. Not to be outdone, nine months later John Derbyshire registered his own version, an imposing winged sphinx in frosted glass. Unfortunately, no connection can be proved between these glass sphinxes and the bronze sphinxes now at the base of the Needle, as the latter were not cast until 1882. The needle itself was reproduced in pressed glass in 1877, a year before it actually reached London, under the guise of 'a jar for pomade or other like substance'. The design was registered by G. V. de Luca of Basinghall Street in the City of London, but the manufacturer is not known.

John Derbyshire's hollow wares show the same inventiveness as his figures. A piano insulator in the form of a mammoth's foot and a vase in the form of a hand, both in a green/yellow glass probably containing uranium, were among his first designs, while in his last year at Salford he produced a successful classical-style spill vase decorated with swags of fruit (cf. fig. 18). Perhaps his two most elaborate designs were a tobacco jar registered in May, 1876, and a conservatory vase of August, 1875. The tobacco jar, which we only know of through drawings, was decorated with figures in panels symbolising the four continents. Only one example of the conservatory vase is known (fig. 16). It is of frosted glass, stands nine inches high, and is decorated with dogs flushing game birds amid sparsely-placed trees. The whole piece has a slight Bohemian flavour.

With the disappearance of John Derbyshire in 1877, much of the interest goes out of Manchester pressed glass. A few decorative pieces in coloured opaline glass (fig. 14) were made in the 1880s by Burtles Tate and Molineaux Webb but the emphasis seems to have been on ordinary tableware in imitation of cut glass. Whole services were produced such as 'The Duchess' by Molineaux Webb (registered 1882). This was illustrated in *Pottery Gazette*[14] and a large comport is now in the City Art Gallery, Manchester.

The final fifty years of the Manchester Glass Industry (1880-1930) have hardly been investigated at all, and the rest of the story is soon told. The Prussia Street Flint Glass Works of Andrew Ker closed about 1887, and its eventual successor, James Bridge and Co., was taken over by Butterworth's in 1895. Percival Vickers (fig. 17) closed in 1914, while Burtles Tate survived until 1924, when it too was absorbed by Butterworth's. Molineaux Webb & Co. was sold by the Webb family in 1931 and finally closed about 1936. From about 1900 scientific glass was produced besides pressed and cut tableware. A poignant letter survives[15], dated 5th June, 1923, from the China and Glass Department of Harrods to Molineaux Webb, in which the sale of some pressed glass is discussed. At the top of the letter a hand has added '31 competitors against us and our lines were successful against the lot'. Butterworth's was the final Manchester firm to close, some time after the Second World War. The factory was featured in *Pottery Gazette* in 1938 and presented a curious mixture of old and new. Its speciality was high-pressure gauge glasses, but at the same time the clay for the pots was still being prepared by kneading with bare feet.

Today there are only street names to show that Manchester ever had a glass industry, and even these are in danger of disappearing. Glass Street in Hulme, for instance, has already been struck from the current Manchester A-Z. However, while the site evidence may be fading, the glass itself is slowly coming to light, re-establishing Manchester's place in the history of English glassmaking.

POSTSCRIPT.

Since this text went to press, the following facts have come to light:-

The decanter shown in fig. 9 was exhibited by Messrs. Phillips and Pearce at the 1867 Paris Universal Exhibition. It is illustrated on p. 67 of the 1867 *Art Journal* and described (p. 93) as "the most skilful and artistic example of engraving in the Exhibition". It was said to be by the same hand as a jug displayed by Mr. J. Dobson," the work of a skilful German engraver, located in England."

With regard to the tumbler engraved by A. Böhm (p. 66), Mrs. Mary Boydell has drawn the author's attention to a ruby coated vase made by the Manchester firm Percival Yates and engraved by Böhm with Richard Coeur de Lion and Saladin at the Battle of Ascalon. This suggests that Böhm did work in Manchester for a time. The vase was exhibited by W. White of Dublin at the Irish Industrial Exhibition of 1853 and described in *The Irish Industrial Exhibition of 1853: a detailed catalogue . . .*, edited by John Sproule, Dublin, 1854, p. 399.

NOTES

1. *Illustrated Catalogue of the Industry of All Nations* (1851 *Art Journal*), p. 290.
2. F. Buckley, 'Old Lancashire Glasshouses', *Journal of the Society of Glass Technology*, XIII, No. 51 (1929), pp. 229-242.
3. H. J. Powell, *Glassmaking in England*, Cambridge University Press (1923), pp. 120, 168.
4. L. M. Angus-Butterworth, *British Table and Ornamental Glass*, London, Leonard Hill (1956), pp. 83-6.
5. For an account of this glasshouse see Ruth Hurst Vose, *Glass*, London, Collins (1980), pp. 143-6.
6. *Pottery Gazette* (July, 1938).
7. Buckley, *op. cit.*, p. 290.
8. The original 'Report of the Proceedings' on the occasion of the presentation of the testimonial is in the City Art Gallery, Manchester. The illuminated address and cigar case are owned by Duncan Webb II's daughter, to whom the author is much indebted for information on the family history.
9. *Art Journal* (1851), p. 290.
10. Information from the Pohl family bible.
11. Another glass jug in the Town Hall collection, engraved with a view of the Town Hall, has recently come to light. The engraving is of good quality and likely to be by Pohl.
12. A photocopy of this letter is in the library at Broadfield House Glass Museum, Kingswinford, the original being in the possession of Mr. H. W. Woodward.
13. George Dodd, *Days at the Factories* (1843), reprinted by EP Publishing Ltd. (1975).
14. *Pottery Gazette Supplement* (1883).
15. In the possession of Duncan Webb II's daughter.

Figure 1. Photograph of Thomas George Webb (1827-1901) who with David Wilkinson became senior partner in the firm of Molineaux Webb on the retirement of Thomas Webb II in 1859.

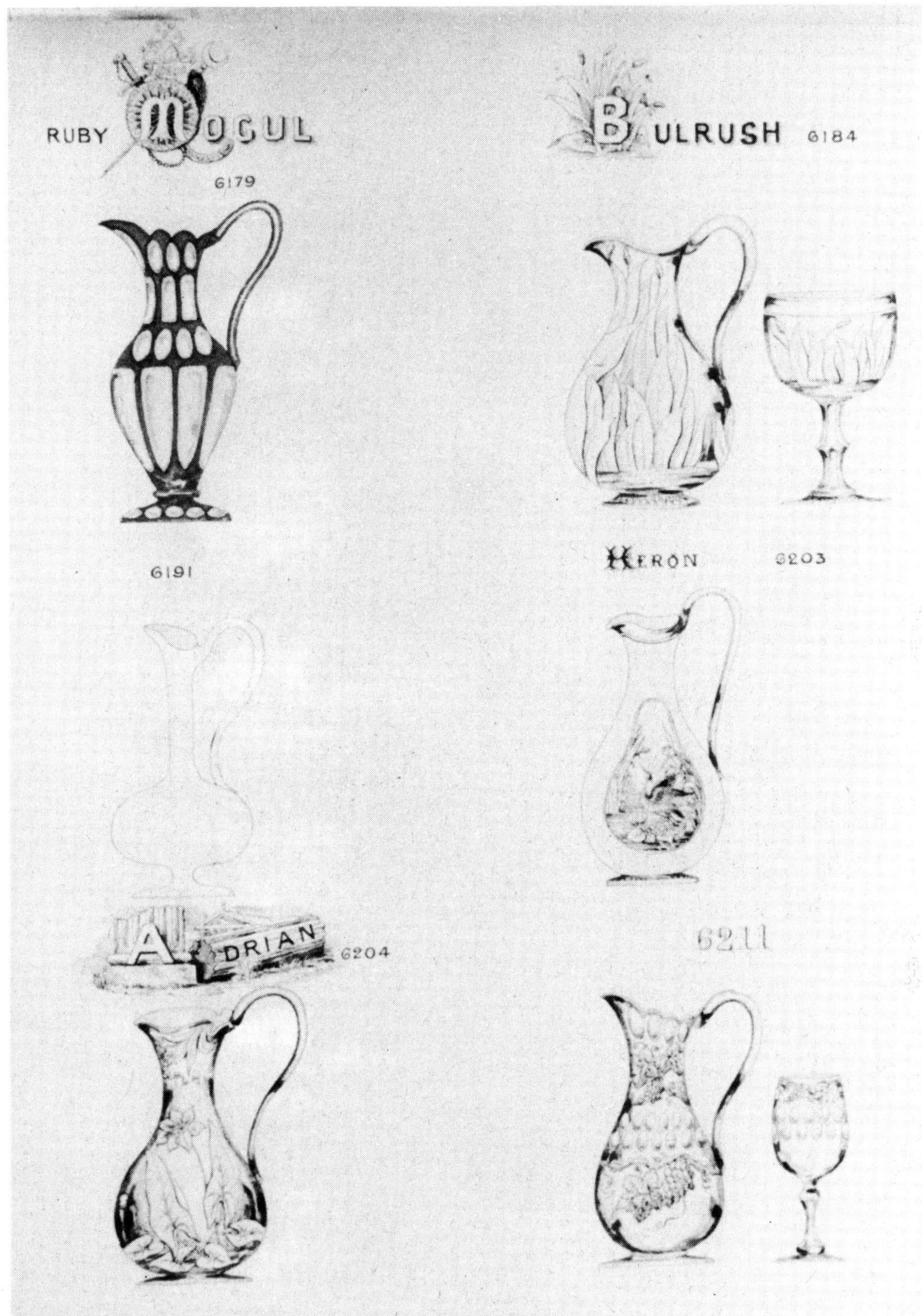

Figure 2. No. 1 Book designs from the Water Jugs and Goblets section of the Molineaux Webb pattern-book, Great Exhibition period (*c*. 1851). City of Manchester Art Galleries.

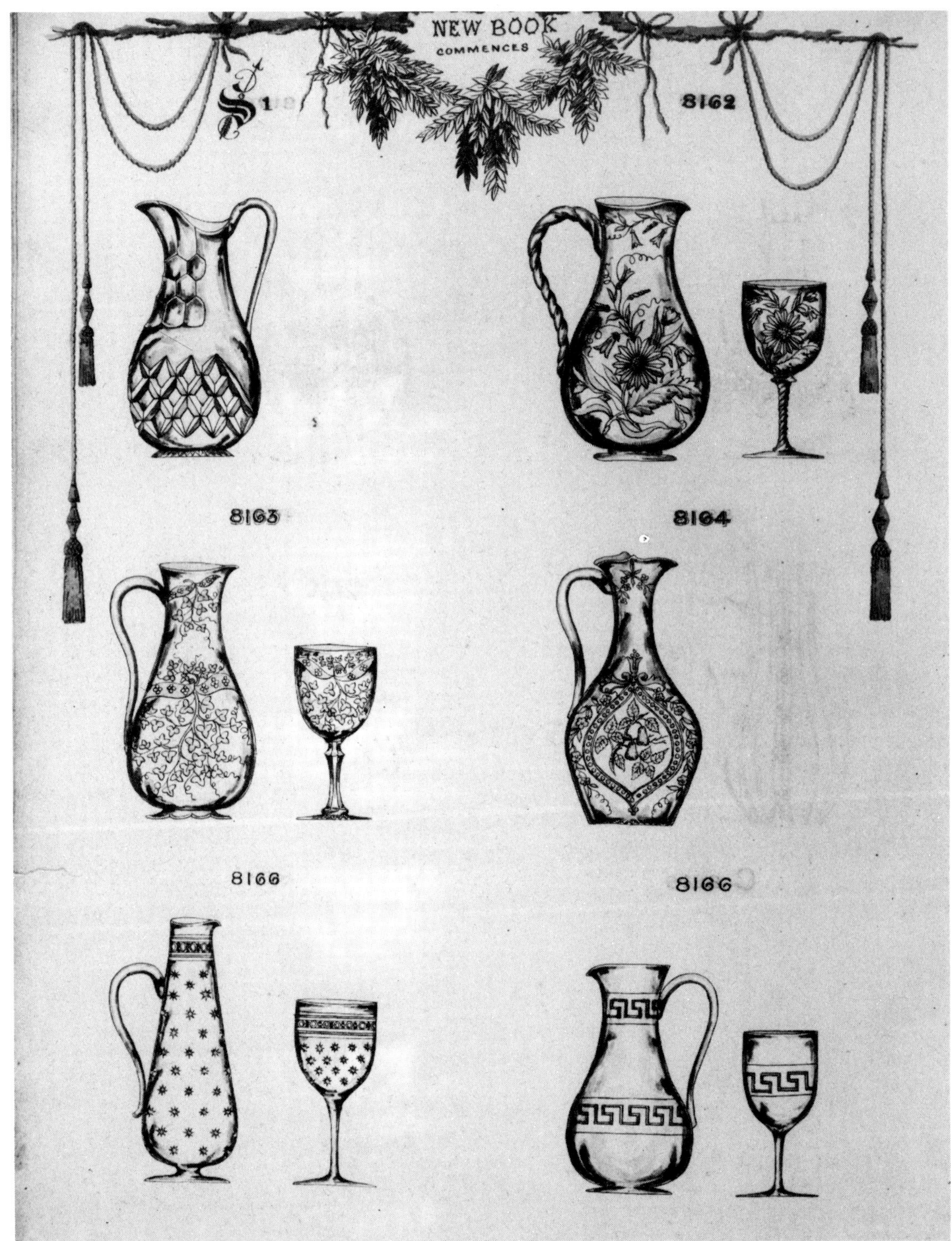

Figure 3. No. 3 or New Book designs from the Water Jugs and Goblets section of the Molineaux Webb pattern-book, dating from the 1860s. City of Manchester Art Galleries.

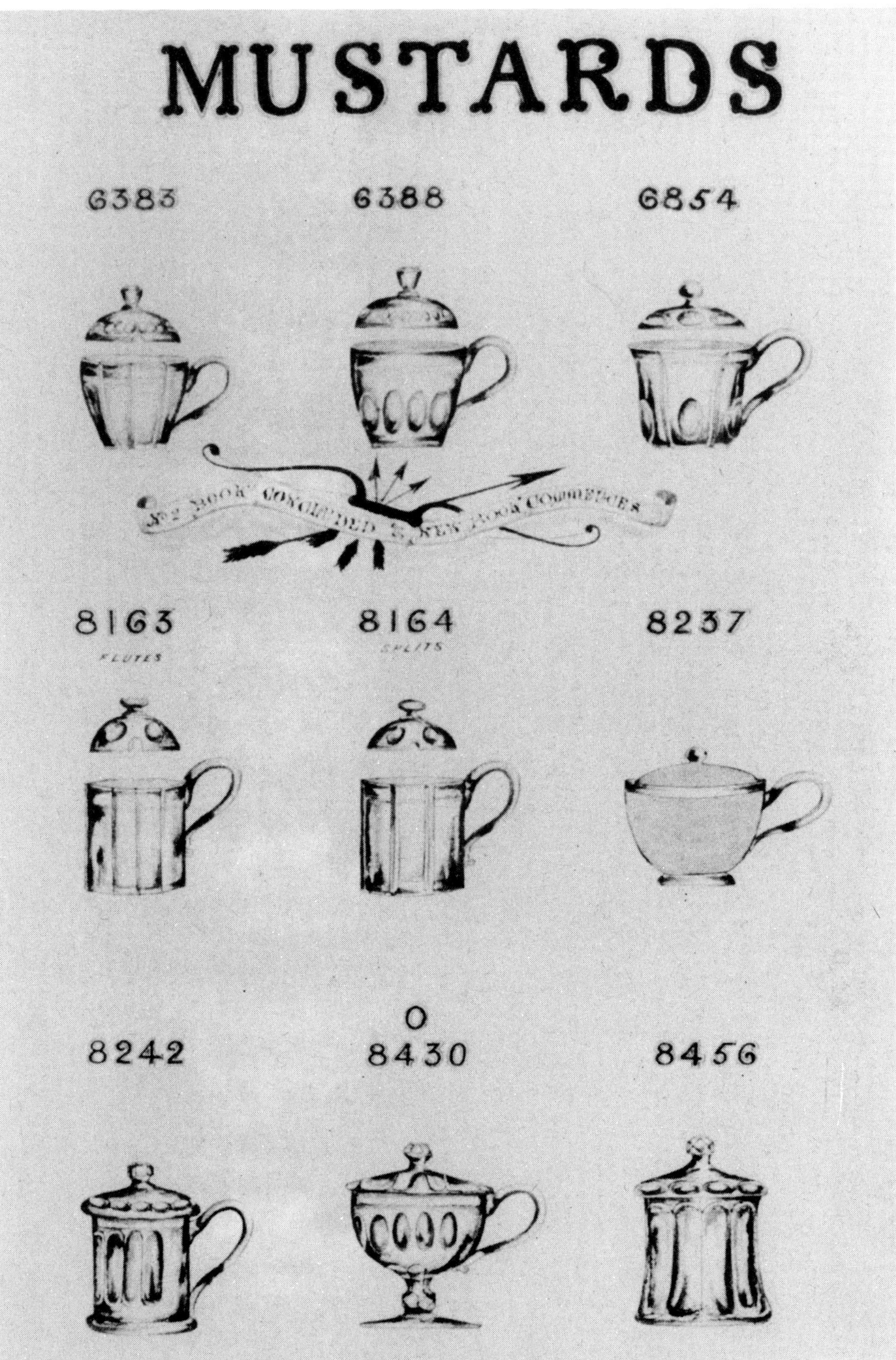

Figure 4. No. 2 and New Book designs for mustard-pots from the Molineaux Webb pattern-book, dating from the 1860s. City of Manchester Art Galleries.

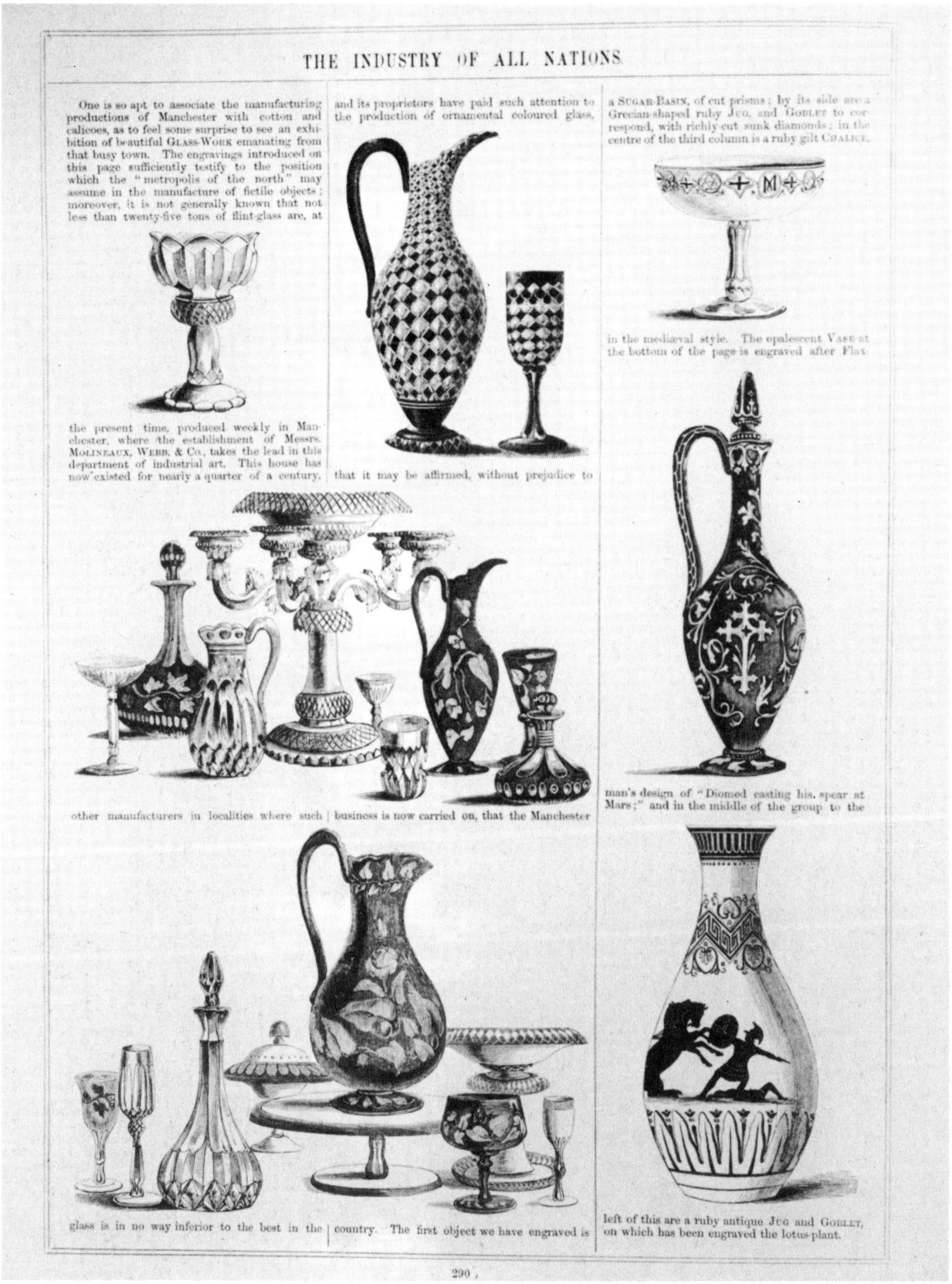

One is so apt to associate the manufacturing productions of Manchester with cotton and calicoes, as to feel some surprise to see an exhibition of beautiful GLASS-WORK emanating from that busy town. The engravings introduced on this page sufficiently testify to the position which the "metropolis of the north" may assume in the manufacture of fictile objects; moreover, it is not generally known that not less than twenty-five tons of flint-glass are, at the present time, produced weekly in Manchester, where the establishment of Messrs. MOLINEAUX, WEBB, & Co., takes the lead in this department of industrial art. This house has now existed for nearly a quarter of a century, and its proprietors have paid such attention to the production of ornamental coloured glass, that it may be affirmed, without prejudice to other manufacturers in localities where such business is now carried on, that the Manchester glass is in no way inferior to the best in the country. The first object we have engraved is a SUGAR-BASIN, of cut prisms; by its side are a Grecian-shaped ruby JUG, and GOBLET to correspond, with richly-cut sunk diamonds; in the centre of the third column is a ruby gilt CHALICE, in the mediæval style. The opalescent VASE at the bottom of the page is engraved after Flaxman's design of "Diomed casting his spear at Mars;" and in the middle of the group to the left of this are a ruby antique JUG and GOBLET, on which has been engraved the lotus-plant.

Figure 5. Page from the 1851 *Art Journal* showing examples of Molineaux Webb's glass at the Great Exhibition.

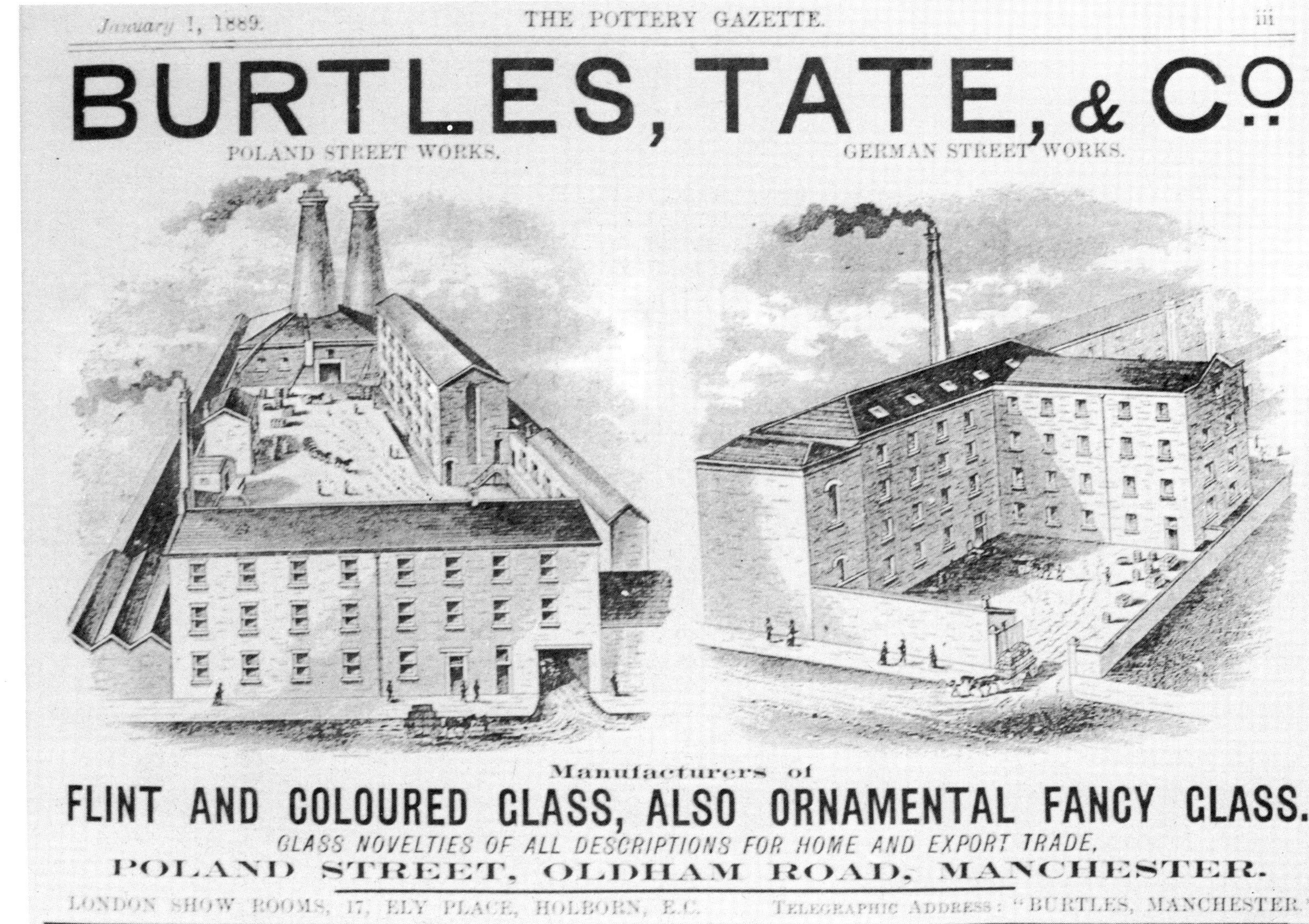

Figure 6. Advertisement from the 1889 *Pottery Gazette* showing Burtles Tate's two works in Ancoats. The firm was founded about 1860 and closed in 1924.

Figure 7. Amber cut decanter corresponding to pattern No. 7085 from the No. 2 book of the decanters section of the pattern book. Molineaux Webb, 1850s. Ht. 12in. (30. 5 cm.). City of Manchester Art Galleries.

Figure 8. Design for amber cut decanter from the Molineaux Webb pattern-book. The design is No. 7085 and comes from the No. 2 book of the decanters section. City of Manchester Art Galleries.

Figure 9. Claret decanter probably by Molineaux Webb, 1860s. Ht. 9½ in. (24.1 cm.). Collection of the great-great-great-granddaughter of Thomas Webb I.

Figure 10. Manchester Town Hall Goblet, made at the Prussia Street Flint Glass Works of Andrew Ker to commemorate the opening of the Town Hall in 1877, and engraved by Wilhelm Pohl. Ht. $15\frac{1}{2}$in. (39.4 cm.). City of Manchester Art Galleries.

Figure 11. John Derbyshire's celebrated paperweight based on the Landseer lions at the foot of Nelson's Column. The design was registered in 1874. Ht. $4\frac{3}{4}$in. (12.1 cm.). Broadfield House Glass Museum.

Figure 12. Lion paperweight in black glass bearing the JD and anchor mark of John Derbyshire but not registered. This version with crossed legs is much less common than that based on the lions at the foot of Nelson's column. L. $6\frac{1}{2}$in. (16.5 cm.). Private Collection.

Figure 13. Neither the frosted figure of Queen Victoria, Ht. $8\frac{1}{2}$in. (21.6), nor the green glass dog, L. $7\frac{1}{2}$in. (19 cm.), are marked but they resemble other John Derbyshire products and were probably made by him or another Manchester factory. Broadfield House Glass Museum.

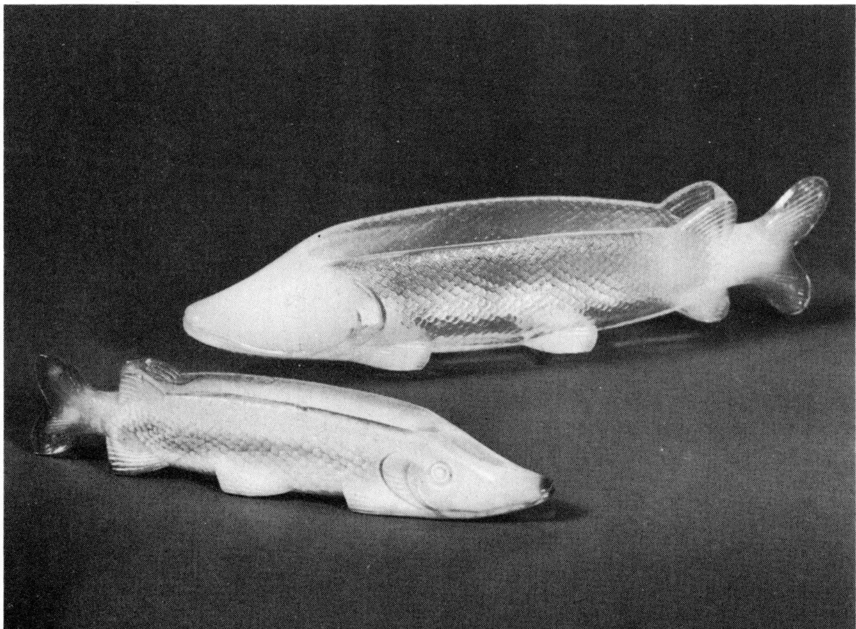

Figure 14. Two pressed glass flower holders in the form of pike. The larger fish, L. 10in. (25.4 cm.), in yellow opalescent glass was registered by Molineaux Webb in 1885, the smaller, L. 6in. (17.8 cm.), is pale blue and unmarked. Broadfield House Glass Museum.

Figure 15. Heavy, pressed drinking glasses, a type that was produced in Manchester and other centres during the second half of the 19th century. Max. Ht. 6in. (15.2 cm.). Author's collection.

Figure 16. Conservatory Vase in frosted glass, registered by John Derbyshire in August 1875. Ht. 9in. (22.9 cm.). City of Manchester Art Galleries.

Figure 17. Small tazza registered by Percival Vickers in 1865. Ht. 4in. (10. 1 cm.). Simplified patterns set against a frosted background were much favoured by the Manchester pressed glass firms. Broadfield House Glass Museum.

Figure 18. Preserve Jar in dark blue glass, registered 21 March, 1877 by the Regent Flint Glass Co., Salford. Ht. 6in. (15. 2 cm.). It does not bear the JD and anchor mark, and indeed after 1876 the name of John Derbyshire disappears. Broadfield House Glass Museum.

The Ricketts family and the Phoenix Glasshouse, Bristol

by CYRIL WEEDEN

A Paper read to the Circle on 19 June, 1980.

The Phoenix glasshouse has always attracted the attention of historians—perhaps disproportionately, some may feel, when compared with other glasshouses in the area. In Bristol there were, over the years, at least sixteen glasshouses (fig. 1), some of which made products of greater historical importance than those of the Phoenix. Indeed, despite an output that spanned a period of over sixty years, there is surprisingly little known about the products of this glasshouse, other than that it made flint glass.[1] H. J. Powell refers to the fact that flint glass of fine quality was made in Bristol and that Henry Ricketts & Co were famous for cut glass, but he adds: 'The patterns were not specially characteristic, and closely resembled the contemporary products of London, Stourbridge and Waterford.'[2] Hugh Owen refers to 'a large goblet, elaborately engraved with Faith, Hope and Charity—the arms of Bristol—several ships and other devices', in the possession of a Mr. Michael Castle.[3] However, the only firm evidence exists in a goblet with an illustration of the Phoenix glasshouse engraved on it, now held by the Bristol City Museum (fig. 2; cf. fig. 3).

Why then has the Phoenix glasshouse received so much credit compared with other Bristol glasshouses? There are perhaps a number of reasons, not the least its name. There is something evocative in the allusion to a mythical bird perpetuating its existence through fire, especially in the case of a glasshouse, where heat is one of the principal factors of production. However, there was nothing novel in the choice of name, since it came from an inn, on the site of which the glasshouse was built. It was the last glasshouse to be built in Bristol, and was one of three that continued long after all the others had closed down. Apart from a glasshouse at Crews Hole it was the only one to be built in Bristol in the second half of the eighteenth century, and records of its activities through the local press are therefore more readily available. More important, a consignment of papers relating to the Ricketts family and their involvement in the glasshouse has been lodged with the Bristol Record Office.[4] Through this source can be traced much of the development of the Phoenix glasshouse, and the personalities of those who ran it.

Again, Hugh Owen's reference to the Phoenix glasshouse has popularised it in the minds of many people. He wrote: 'In the year 1785 a large flint-glass manufactory was commenced at Temple Gate, by Messrs James and George Taylor, the premises which were previously the "Phoenix" Inn; and from that circumstance it was called the Phoenix Glass Works. Messrs Ricketts and Co., succeeded to the business in August 1789, . . .'[5] The Taylors were experienced glassmakers, having manufactured crown glass for at least three generations, if not more. In 1752 they leased a glasshouse in Red Lane, opposite Temple Gate,[6] previously believed to have been worked by Benjamin Perrott, himself a crown glass manufacturer. In 1783 the then current partnership between Samuel, James and George Taylor was dissolved,[7] and the Red Lane glasshouse probably ceased production.

The Perrott family seems to have owned or leased much of the property around Temple Gate. Humphrey, the brother of Benjamin Perrott, worked a glasshouse in Temple Street, close to the junction with Portwall Lane, and in 1759 a John Standford Perrott assigned premises and land, including the Phoenix Inn, to Daniel Taylor.[8] In 1788, Elizabeth Taylor, widow of Samuel, leased the Phoenix Inn and property relating to it to Jacob Wilcox Ricketts and John Roach.[9] The following year an agreement was reached, as follows,

> '. . . The said John Wadham, Richard Ricketts, Jacob Wilcox Ricketts, David Evans, Richard Symes and Thomas Morgan did . . . in the year of our Lord One Thousand Seven Hundred and Eighty Nine enter into Copartnership together in the Trade or Business of Flint Glass Manufacturers under the firm of Wadham Ricketts and Company and for the purpose of carrying on their said Trade did purchase a certain Messuage, Tenement or Inn known by the name of Phoenix, situate near Temple Gate . . . which purchase was made with moneys belonging to the said Copartnership but the said premises were conveyed unto the said Jacob Wilcox Ricketts alone and whereas the said John Wadham, Richard Ricketts, Jacob Wilcox Ricketts, David Evans, Richard Symes and Thomas Morgan did erect and build in and upon the yard belonging to the said Phoenix Inn a Flint Glass House . . . '[10]

This, of course, contradicts the statement made by Hugh Owen, but in a sense it is not surprising. The Taylors were skilled in making crown glass[11] and glassmakers tended to keep to their specialities—indeed, during the days of the Excise Tax they were under pressure to do so. There seems to be no reason why James and George Taylor, nearing the close of their careers as crown glass makers, should suddenly turn to the manufacturing of flint glass.

Since the agreement specifies that the premises were conveyed to Jacob Wilcox Ricketts alone we can assume that he was the moving force behind the venture. Jacob Wilcox Ricketts (fig. 4) was by all accounts a flamboyant character, and a man of strong views. Son of a tobacconist, he had already started his own tobacco business,[12] whilst he in 1788, at the age of 35, had with Philip George founded the Bristol Porter Brewery, soon to be the largest brewery in the city.[13] Later he was to establish the Castle Bank.[14] Jacob Wilcox Ricketts was an entrepreneur from the classic mould, and for his glass venture he attracted an influential group of people around him, of whom David Evans, later to be sheriff and then mayor of Bristol,[15] was probably the most important.

The Phoenix glasshouse was soon in business, and from August 22nd to October 10th, 1789, the following notice appeared in Felix Farley's *Bristol Journal:*

> 'Phoenix Flint Glass House Wadham, Ricketts and Co. at the Phoenix Flint Glass-House, without Temple Gate, Bristol (late the Phoenix Inn) most respectfully inform their friends and the Public, that they have begun to work said Glass-house; where will be kept a complete assortment of every article of flint glass, which will be sold on the most reasonable terms.'

It would be interesting to know why Jacob Wilcox Ricketts chose, or was persuaded to choose, flint glassmaking as a venture. For risk investment the times were scarcely propitious. Since 1745 the glass industry had been subject to an excise tax which, in order to pay for the Government's military commitments, had more than doubled in the ten years preceding the building of the Phoenix glasshouse. Furthermore, the principal cause of the increase, the American War of Independence, not only affected one of the traditional and most lucrative of Bristol markets, but also lessened the advantage of the drawback on exported goods, the only tax relief afforded to manufacturers. Thus, the British flint glass trade had been in the doldrums for most of the 1780s, although there were signs of revival toward the end of the decade, and this may have been the cause of optimism.[16]

Of the thirteen glasshouses at work in Bristol at this time three made flint glass, and a new venture would have been viewed with some concern by those already in the market. The Phoenix was, after all, the only flint glasshouse to have been built in Bristol for well over fifty years. Experienced glassmakers and decorators would be needed, and the new concern would have had to import them from other flint glass manufacturing areas such as London, Stourbridge or Newcastle; or poach them from local manufacturers.

One of the Bristol flint glasshouses, that at Bedminster, seems to have been on the point of closing down, and may well have done so by the time the Phoenix glasshouse commenced production. Prior knowledge of this may well have encouraged the Ricketts consortium to go ahead with their venture, since this glasshouse would have provided a source of skilled labour; but this is speculation. A second flint glasshouse was sited on the corner of Portwall Lane and Temple Street, facing the Phoenix. In 1786 the partnership that ran this glasshouse terminated their agreement, leaving it in the hands of Richard Cannington.[17] Three years later he sold out to a new consortium consisting of James Jones, a merchant and also proprietor of the Crews Hole glasshouse, John Mayo Tandey, a former employee of Vigor, Stevens and Company, who made flint glass at Redcliff Backs and crown glass at Thomas Street, and William Fry, then in business as a distiller and wine merchant.[18] Although James Jones's experience lay in bottle making and John Mayo Tandey's in crown glass, the Temple Street glasshouse continued with flint glass. The third flint glasshouse, that of Vigor, Stevens and Company, was in financial difficulties at this time, and it is unlikely that it welcomed the revival of the Temple Street glasshouse, and even less so the entry of the Phoenix glasshouse into the trade. Some measure of the feeling that existed may be gauged from the notice that appeared when John Mayo Tandey and two of his colleagues joined the other concerns:

> 'Messrs Vigor, Stevens and Company of this city, glass-makers and copartners, do hereby apprize their friends and the public that John Thomas and Matthew Hill late clerks at their Flint Glass Manufactory on Redcliff Backs and John Mayo Tandey, late clerk at their Crown Glass Manufactory in St. Thomas Street, have been for some time past dismissed from their respective employments'.[19]

To which there were spirited replies from all three on somewhat similar lines:

> 'Mr John Thomas presents his most cordial respects to Messrs Vigor, Stevens, Randolph and Stevens, and is highly obliged to them for their unkind advertisement in the Bristol

Gazette of the 16th Instant after so many years of faithful service. He is now established in the Phoenix Glass-House Temple Gate carried on by Wadham Ricketts and Co.'[20]

In 1791, the Temple Street and the Phoenix glasshouses amalgamated, with William Fry and James Jones joining the Phoenix partnership, and John Mayo Tandey surrendering his interest. The Temple Street site was leased to John Hawkins, James Ewer and John Ambrose, woollen draper, hatter and grocer respectively,[21] presumably for purposes other than glass manufacturing, since it is unlikely that the Phoenix glasshouse partnership would have encouraged competition. At that time the glass trade was once more in the doldrums, and that presumably was the reason behind the closure. From 1792, however, trade began to improve, despite the increase to 20% in the general duty imposed by America on imported glassware in 1794.[22]

As trade expanded, so the partnership contracted. By 1796 Richard Symes, Thomas Morgan and John Wadham had withdrawn, and James Jones had died, whilst William Fry had been declared a bankrupt.[23] The partnership now consisted of Jacob Wilcox Ricketts, his brother Richard, and David Evans. In the meantime, Vigor, Stevens and Company were recovering from their financial problems, which had been caused by the untimely death of Robert Vigor in 1782, drowned while watering his horse at a pond.[24] This, seemingly, removed the stabilizing element, for the concern, after many years of profitability, immediately began to lose money to the extent of £35,000 over the next fourteen years.[25] Recovery came when it was taken over in 1795 by two of the most influential businessmen in the city, George Daubeny and John Cave. George Daubeny was the third, and arguably the most successful, of the four members of the family bearing the same name who, in successive generations, took it from small shopkeeping to a commercial distinction that ranked it among the leading merchant families in the city of Bristol.[26] John Cave, equally eminent in Bristol commercial life, was a close friend of Daubeny, and had nominated him as candidate for Parliament. Together they had helped to found the banking firm of Ames, Cave and Company,[27] and this could be the reason why they were anxious to keep the Redcliff Backs glasshouse in production. Although there is no evidence to the effect, it is conceivable that they were protecting their financial interests. John Cave died in 1800 and was succeeded by his son John, who also became a Bristol citizen of some substance.

On February 6th, 1802, the Redcliff Backs and the Phoenix glasshouses amalgamated and under the terms of the agreement the flint glasshouse and the crown glasshouse in Thomas Street closed down. The agreement reached by George Daubeny and John Cave reads:

> ' . . . we have now removed our Manufactory of Flint Glass to Temple Gate and by joining ourselves in Copartnership with Ricketts & Evans have considerably augmented our works in the Flint Bottle Trade'.[28]

A corresponding notice was published by the Phoenix proprietors, together with the advice that Richard Ricketts had retired from the company 'on the 1st June last'.[29] He was replaced by J. W. Ricketts' son Henry. The notice then went on to state 'that in future the firm will be Ricketts Evans and Phoenix Glass Company'. This was in fact the first time that the term Phoenix had appeared in the name of the company, although the glasshouse had always been described in that way. The first notice confirms that the Redcliff Backs glasshouse made flint bottles, but it is not clear whether flint domestic glassware was manufactured there. The Phoenix glasshouse seems to have made both, for the announcement when it opened stated: 'where will be kept a complete assortment of every article of flint-glass'.

In 1811 the business moved into the manufacture of common bottles by leasing a glasshouse in Cheese Lane, or Avon Street, as this particular site was later termed.[30] This meant that, with the exception of window glass, the concern could now offer a full range of glassware, and through J. W. Ricketts' share in the Bristol Porter Brewery it had a tied market in bottles. By now, of the eleven glasshouses that were working when the Phoenix glasshouse was built, three only were still in use; a bottle glasshouse in Limekiln Lane, run by J. Nicholas; the bottle glasshouse taken over by the Phoenix consortium; and another adjacent to it in Avon Street, owned by Joseph and Septimus Cookson, sons of Isaac Cookson, then in business as a bottle maker in Newcastle. Crown glass, although manufactured at Nailsea, was no longer made at Bristol.

Up to this point there is little evidence on which to base an assessment of the fortunes of the concern. In 1792, when Richard Symes withdrew, he received the sum of £1,200 which, since the partners had equal shares, places the total capital at £9,600, and this is substantiated when Thomas Morgan withdrew the following year and received £1,371.8.7. In January 1795, however, John Wadham's share was assessed at the lower figure of £1,100; and later, in September, that of William Fry, now bankrupt, at £935. 15. 3. If it assumed that the partners bore trading losses by readjusting their share capital, then they had run into problems. By 1798 it would seem that the position had to an extent recovered since in that year James Jones's executors were paid £1,623. 8. 0. When George Daubeny died in 1806 his executors received £8,834. 11. 3., which, even though the terms of the amalgamation are not known, indicated continued success in the subsequent decade.[31] This could well have been the case, since the fluctuations follow closely the pattern of the flint glass trade for the period.

Despite the withdrawals from the partnership there is no evidence that there were personal problems, certainly not within the Ricketts family. On the contrary, the early relationship between Jacob Wilcox Ricketts and his son must have been very good. He was generous to Henry, giving him a gift of £500 on his marriage in 1805, and a further £1,000 on his becoming a partner at the glasshouse.[32] They were partners also in the Bristol Porter Brewery Company. A dynasty, if such was in J. W. Ricketts' mind, appeared to be well founded. The trading difficulties of the early years had given way to a recovery which brought the partners an average return on their investment of ten per cent a year, which they ploughed back into the business. Following the death of David Evans in 1816, his estate received £18,794,[33] which indicates a remarkable degree of success, However, by 1820 the record profit of £7,200 in 1818 had plummeted to a record loss of £7,122, and the concern continued to lose money for the next three years at least, and possibly longer.[34] By now the partnership consisted of J. W. Ricketts, his son Henry and John Cave.

The first indication that the relationship between Henry Ricketts and his father was strained comes from a note signed 'S. Stephens'. J. W. Ricketts is pressing a Mr Bickley[35] for a debt and Henry is asked to intervene.[36] He does so, not directly, but through his brother Alfred and receives the following reply:

> 'I cannot obtain a direct answer from Father, whether he will or will not, make application in writing for the Money—his reply was, 'I may well Sir, I may well. I'll see whether I can have my Money'—under such circumstances I am at a loss to say how you are to act—your own discretion will best dictate to you'.

J. W. Ricketts was evidently a man to be treated circumspectly and Henry Ricketts seems often to have corresponded with him through a third party. It is again S. Stephens who informs Henry that his father proposed to retire from the 'glass concern', and that he wished to transfer his interest to Alfred, and to receive an annuity of £500 a year. This was too much for Henry, who was prepared to accept the former condition, but not the latter; to which his father replies, 'he thought himself from his having been one of the formers of the Business, and from his long continuance in it fully entitled to the sum he had required'. These exchanges took place in the first fortnight of August, 1820, and a week later came the sharpest of replies:

> 'J. W. Ricketts love to his son Henry—having to inform him, another time (than next Sunday) would be more agreeable to see him, and Mrs Henry to Dinner, while Mrs Winwood is under my care—I shall endeavour to keep her as quiet as possible—its the particular request of (Dr Stock)'.

In October Henry Ricketts announced his intention of relinquishing the management of the concern. Later in the month John Cave wrote to the effect: 'your Brother Alfred will not accept the offer. We must go on as we are at present'. Whether Alfred was asked to manage the concern, or to replace J. W. Ricketts, as was suggested, is not disclosed, but by June the following year Henry Ricketts had agreed to continue. By September, 1821, John Cave had had enough and offered his resignation, adding, in his letter to Henry: 'it is very unpleasant for me to witness the difference still subsisting between a Father and a Son'. Much of the dispute between Henry Ricketts and his father seems to have turned on the fact that documents were not available to Jacob Wilcox Ricketts for inspection, and John Cave makes this point to Henry, adding that his father had made: 'many severe observations on your conduct as Manager of the Concern'. He discloses that J. W. Ricketts had threatened to have the company dissolved, but had changed this to an offer of his share at £16,000. 'My reply was that I would much rather sell my share at the sum offered'. However, he suggests to Henry Ricketts that the offer should be carefully considered, adding that: 'if we should now think it in our interest to accept this offer, arrangements respecting a new Concern can soon be fixed'.

John Cave's pressure on Henry seems to have prompted him to write a conciliatory letter to his father in which he offers to make the books available. He suggests they could resolve their differences if his father would 'enter into any or every subject coolly'; the final word is underlined, perhaps emphasising Henry's assessment of his father's temperament. There is a clue in the letter as to the reasons underlying Henry Ricketts' actions: 'you have said there have been those who have vilified my conduct—one a gentleman—the other the writer of an anonymous letter—I have solemnly declared to you that until both were produced I would never produce my cash book'. He accepts, however, that the letter has been destroyed, and therefore no longer considers it an obstacle to their reconciliation. He refers to his father's wish to retire from the concern, comments that he would rather retire himself, but states his preference for the concern to continue 'upon a basis to prevent a recurrence of our unhappy division'. This long letter ends on an emotional note, 'Whether I am now to meet you as a Son wishes to meet a Father, and as a Father and Son ought to meet, in the spirit of duty, affection and solicitude, is for you alone to determine. The time passing over us will wait for no compromise—we can be but shortly together—let that period be one of domestic bliss—whether I shall be called to attend the dying pillow of a parent, or you of a son, is not for us to know—let not however the period of the existence of our differences wait for that hour which God alone knows may not be permitted to be employed in a union upon earth—that our lives henceforth may be spent in that harmony which till within these three years they were in the undisturbed possession, I feel as your son, most anxious'. But, in so far as Jacob Wilcox and Henry were concerned, the Ricketts were constitutionally sound, and the fell sergeant was therefore not so strict in his arrest.

But what was the cause of the quarrel? Despite the many letters there is no clear reason. There are hints: 'until our reconciliation is effected, I forbear entering fully upon this subject, in the mean while let me assure you that the whole family of the Ushers[37] dread that a reconciliation should be effected—it is in their interest it should be otherwise—the ingratitude I have experienced from that family has been such, that I will never pass over'. This reference is tantalizingly vague and appears again only in Henry Ricketts' ledger.[38] In 1815 and again in 1836 he conducted a small amount of business with a Joseph S. Usher, against whose name, in the creditor column is written in pencil—'bad'. It must therefore be left to speculation as to why a father who could write to his son in 1802 as follows: 'it gave me great pleasure to find you was well and in perfect safety so far on your journey—and may the Allmighty allways protect you has he have all ready done for which we cannot be to thankfull'[39]; a man who could take his son as a partner, both in the glasshouse and the brewery, appoint him manager of the former and, when his senior partner died in 1816, allow the concern to take his son's name—how he could then, within the next two to three years, quarrel with him so bitterly. A point which may have had a bearing on the matter is that Jacob Wilcox Ricketts' brother Richard, who had been associated with the development of the Phoenix glasshouse, died in 1818.[40] From the evidence it could be suspected that J. W. Ricketts' favourite occupations were reading balance sheets, collecting debts and making money, but had he an emotional side that caused him to grieve his brother's death, and possibly impaired his judgement? Henry Ricketts, who had married Richard's daughter Elisabeth[41], appeals to his father: 'the tie existing between us is not merely that of a parent and a son it is also between the only child of a deceased brother. . . and also our little children! such is the effect of family discord' (*sic*).

The dispute clearly affected the family, and two of his sisters attempted to effect a reconciliation. Mathilda was direct and to the point. She wrote to say that she had mentioned Henry's intention to call on Sunday. J. W. Ricketts' answer was equally to the point: 'he hoped not, any third day in the week you know where to find him, and he did not wish to have his mind disturbed on that day'. Hannah, the Mrs Winwood mentioned in Jacob Wilcox Ricketts' earlier letter, was more cautious. She wrote to say that she had been to see their father, who had heard her with 'more patience than I expected'. She continued: 'he conversed with great coolness and told me not to make myself uneasy about it . . . I said all that I could think of to induce him to be friends and sincerely wish and think, that I have done some little good and that we shall be soon all good friends together for of nothing have I greater dread than family quarrels'.

But J. W. Ricketts was obdurate and Henry, receiving no reply to his letter, was forced some six weeks later[42] to write once more protesting that he was still in ignorance of the cause of the quarrel. He pleads: 'why do I receive a treatment which I feel undeserved of—If you treated me with the natural affection of a parent for six and Thirty Years, and then for the first time feel offended, why should the succeeding three years pass over us without a reconciliation'. The letter is punctuated with variation of mood: 'the vilest criminal cannot receive more severe treatment', followed by a flash of intransigence: 'but wherein did our differences commence . . . I do solemnly assure you only in an imagination of wrong done to you, in what I have so repeatedly intreated you to search into and you will find yourself in error'.

The year 1820 was a bad one both for the flint glass and the glass bottle trades, the former falling 21%, and the latter 29%, below the peak year of 1818 (fig. 5). In a letter to his father, Henry Ricketts explains in part the reasons for the massive financial loss sustained by the Phoenix glasshouse that year. He writes: 'the Glass Makers were at work but every alternate week for a considerable time throughout the year, and even during that period instead of filling 8 to 9 pots, it was only an average of from 4 to 5 pots—the Bottle works in similar proportion and the cutting shop three days in a week and that too with a short complement of hands—nor does this statement apply to the last year only, but to the year preceding—the Excise too being so particularly strict and the mode adopted so altered as to increase the expense of the work by an additional number of hands employed'.[43] The losses of 1820/21 brought to an end a remarkably profitable run by the Phoenix glasshouse. In the twelve years between Henry Ricketts' taking over and the start of the quarrel with his father the annual profits of the concern averaged £3, 780.[44] His management can scarcely have been the cause of the quarrel, but from 1820 the losses were to continue for at least a further three years and no doubt this impeded a reconciliation.

In 1821 Henry Ricketts published a patent entitled: 'An Improvement in the Art or Method of Making or Manufacturing Glass Bottles, such as are used for Wine, Porter, Beer, or Cyder',[45] and in so doing ensured a permanent place for himself in the history of the glass industry. To appreciate fully the significance of Henry Ricketts' patent one must compare the then current requirements of the wine bottling, brewing and distilling industries with the method by which bottles were made. Drinks containing alcohol were highly taxed, and those engaged in such trades, including Henry Ricketts and his father, had no wish to see bottles overfilled with a product on which they had already paid a heavy duty. Variations in capacity, however, were difficult to avoid with a product that relied so heavily on the judgement and ability of individual glassmakers. Glassmaking was a craft industry in which the glassmaker, after gathering glass on the end of a blowing iron, created a product by his skill in blowing and shaping it with simple tools. By the early nineteenth century the only step toward mechanisation had been in the use of moulds, by which means basic shapes were blown or pressed. In bottle making the moulds were simple in operation and the cavity in most cases was cylindrical, or near-cylindrical, in shape. Having gathered glass on his blowing iron the glassmaker formed it into a cylindrical shape by rolling it on a flat stone or cast iron surface. Then, holding the blowing iron in a vertical position, he lowered the glass into the aperture of the mould and blew until it filled the cavity (fig. 6). The mould formed the side walls of the bottle, but the glassmaker had to judge when he had exerted sufficient pressure to fill the cavity and form the shoulder, which was not constrained by the mould. He then withdrew the blown glass, and a rod ('pontil'), similar in shape and length to the blowing iron, but solid, was attached to the base of the bottle. The blowing iron was cracked off and by manipulating the bottle on the rod the neck was finished by adding a small amount of glass and shaping it with a tool. Moulds were either one-piece, that is near-cylindrical, with the base diameter slightly less than that at the top, thus enabling the bottle to be withdrawn, or two-piece and hinged, in which case the sides of the cavity could be parallel.

Ricketts innovation was the introduction of shoulders to the mould. By this means, he claimed, 'the circumference and diameter of bottles are formed nearly cylindrical, and their height determined so as to contain given quantities or proportions of a wine or beer gallon measure, with a greater degree of regularity or conformity to each other, and all the bottles so made by me after this method present a superior neatness of appearance and regularity of shape for convenient and safe stowage, which cannot by other means be so well attained'. A further claim was that by placing rings of varying thickness at the bottom of the mould the body of the mould would be shortened or increased and hence various sizes of bottles produced.

The importance of this development should not be underrated. This was the first application of machinery to the glass bottle industry,[46] other than the use of simple moulds; and, subsequent refinements apart, it became and remained an important method of making mouth-blown bottles. Why then did not Henry Ricketts apply the inventiveness of which he appeared to be capable to other aspects of bottle making—in particular, to the development of a machine that would dispense with the glass blower ? He does not appear to have tried any further and another fifty years were to pass before the first machine began to find its way into the glassworks, and then it was the invention of a Yorkshireman.

Was Henry Ricketts' preoccupation with his invention the cause of the dispute with his father ? There is no evidence that this was so. In the correspondence there is one reference only to the invention, and that in a letter from John Cave to

Henry Ricketts. He writes: 'I can see no objection to the expenditure of £135 to take out the patent, provided the sale could be increased to pay soon the expense of it, I should almost doubt the propriety of granting a Patent for so trifling an improvement, yet it is in our interest to obtain it'.[47]

The successful years had encouraged the partners to plough back their profits and by 1820 the share capital stood at £64, 622. It is interesting also to see from the accounts of the concern that the value of the buildings between the years 1817 and 1820 increased from £5, 500 to £9, 000. At the same time investment in utensils for flint glassmaking increased from £400 to £2, 150, and for bottle making from £300 to £1, 400.[48] These were increases of some magnitude and pose the question on what the money was spent. Dr Alford suggests that the buoyancy of the market encouraged the partners to increase the capacity of the glasshouses.[49] This could have been achieved in various ways—for example, by installing larger furnaces, employing more labour and by working additional shifts—but the physical constraints of the glasshouses would have imposed limitations on these options. In 1817 the Phoenix concern consisted of two glasshouses, a freehold property at Temple Gate and a leasehold property in Avon Street. During the development of the concern three additional glasshouses had been acquired and closed down, John Cave's glasshouses on Redcliff Backs and in St Thomas Street, and Cannington's old glasshouse in Temple Street. Furthermore, by 1817 there were probably seven other glasshouses not in work. The magnitude of the investment suggests that glassmaking was recommenced in one or more of the idle glasshouses, although there is no firm evidence that this was so. If this were the case then the choice may well have fallen on the Temple Street glasshouse, which had always been used for flint glass, and on the companion glasshouse to the one already leased in Avon Street, which was a bottle glasshouse. Both of the Avon Street glasshouses were owned by John Hilhouse Wilcox, and the lease, signed in 1811, referred to the fact that the second glasshouse was then not working.[50] There is, however, a further possibility. In 1803, to help meet the cost of the war with France, the Government had introduced a tax on profits, and this was repealed in 1816.[51] Profit or loss at the Phoenix glasshouse was determined by the balance between assets and liabilities, and it was therefore very much in the interests of the partners that the value of the buildings and equipment be kept as low as possible. With the tax removed, the partners were able to write in a more realistic figure which, subsequently, helped to cushion the substantial losses that were to occur from 1820 onwards.

Henry Ricketts' bottle patent was not the first venture into the field of invention on the part of the Phoenix concern. On June 5th, 1802, the following notice appeared:

> 'Having discovered an improved method of making all kinds of Glass by which the process is effected in a period of time very much shorter than by the usual mode, and thus created a saving of fuel. Any gentleman in the trade may have my permission to adopt the said improvements on liberal terms. Apply to me at Ricketts Evans & Co's Patent Glass House, Bristol. John Donaldson.'[52]

John Cave's notes relating to the profits of the concern from 1802 to 1807 refer to John Donaldson as manager and partner, receiving a one-eighth share of the profits.[53] When George Daubeny died in 1806 the share was raised to one-sixth, but John Donaldson died the following year, at which point Henry Ricketts took over the management.

Unfortunately, the confidence of the partners in the buoyancy of the market was not justified by events. From 1807 to 1812 bottle sales exceeded those of all previous years, but the doubling of the excise duties and the onset of the Anglo-American war caused sales to fall by about one-third in 1813, from which point they slowly climbed to regain their previous peak, only to fall precipitously again in 1818. Sales of flint glass, which had also been high since the turn of the century, followed a very similar pattern. These variations in sales seem to have been closely linked with the exportation of glass, particularly to the West Indies and the Americas. Economic depression in America in 1819 and the following year, together with the determined attempt of the young government to protect its emerging glass industry, made trading very difficult for the UK glassmakers, in particular those in Bristol, with their strong traditional contacts with the western world. John Cave, in his letter consenting to the payment for the patent comments: 'as to the exports to the West Indies being small I am surprised the Planters are able to pay for any thing during the low price of sugars'. In sending the accounts for 1823/4 to J. W. Ricketts, he adds, 'the trade is at present not worth following.'[54] The concern continued to lose money up to 1823/4, which is the final year of the series of detailed accounts, and in each of the four financial years from 1820 there are references to the bad debts from which the concern suffered; and in 1820 and again in 1823, to the reduction in prices that had to be made. For 1820/21, for example, the note reads: 'Bad Debts this year £8, 275. 16. 5.'. This was about £1,000 more than the trading loss for that year. But they survived, and this may have been due to the change in the duty on flint glass in 1825, which in effect more than halved the rate. Certainly the sales of flint glass responded, and the upward trend accelerated.

The quarrel between J. W. Ricketts and Henry was finally resolved by John Cave, who seems to have played a conciliatory role throughout the sorry affair. He emerges as the one person capable of making a calm and rational approach to the problem, and it was probably due to his efforts that the concern kept going. John Cave brought the matter to a head with a letter to each of his partners in which he stated that he wished to relinquish his interests in the concern as from 30th June, 1825 (fig. 7). It was unlikely that even J. W. Ricketts would have wished to cross swords with John Cave, and neither he nor Henry Ricketts would want to lose so important and influential a partner. Previously Master of the Merchant Venturers, John Cave was by now a member of the Corporation and had been Sheriff in 1822/3. The letter precipitated a decision and possibly that was its intention. Two days following its receipt Jacob Wilcox Ricketts informed his partners that his association with them 'shall be dissolved on 30th June 1825' (fig. 8). One detects a sigh of relief in the letter from the attorneys, Stephens and Goodchild, to Henry Ricketts, dated 14th July, 1825: 'we are rejoiced that this unpleasant business is terminated and shall feel pleasure in waiting on you at any time you may appoint in order to receive instructions'.[55] So Jacob Wilcox Ricketts severed his connection with the glasshouse he had founded some thirty-six years earlier. His share was estimated to be worth £22, 291, which Henry Ricketts and John Cave took over in equal parts, and for which they agreed to pay £21, 500 in four years by equal instalments.[56]

It could be said that the story of the Phoenix glasshouse ended when Jacob Wilcox Ricketts retired, since from that point onwards the concern seems to have gone into a gradual decline. But that would be too simple a statement, since the cause of the decline was complex and far beyond the control of an entrepreneur, however gifted. A number of factors contributed to the decline of the glass industry in Bristol, a decline from which it was never to recover. Whilst this is not the place to detail the causes it is necessary to provide a summary, if only to account for the demise of the Phoenix glasshouse. They can be segregated into three groups:—those due to the vagaries of trade; those due to technological change; those self-inflicted. The eighteenth and early nineteenth centuries were marked by wars, and wars interfere with trade and cost money. To pay for them the glass industry, amongst others, was heavily taxed and, even though there was a drawback on exports, such trade was subject to fluctuation. Sales slumped during the American war of independence, and again during the war with France. From the point of view of Bristol, with its dependence on trade with North America, the West Indies and the Caribbean, the most serious event was the Anglo-American war, which, coupled with the war in Europe, led to violent fluctuations in the sales of all glassware. It was during the latter half of the eighteenth century that technological change began to affect Bristol industry and commerce and, during the following century, the tempo increased. The heart of industrial development was beginning to settle in the midlands and the north of England. Coal, the basis for the energy that was needed in increasing quantities to power industry, was more accessible in south Yorkshire and Lancashire, and a network of canals began to provide effective links between the factories and the ports. Bristol, with the Avon Gorge between its harbour and the sea, was not so well placed. Prevarication held up the development of a tide-free harbour, and left Bristol a century behind its rival Liverpool. A similar criticism could be levelled at the direct river and canal link with London, which came too late to influence Bristol trade.[57]

It is surprising that a man with as much business acumen as Jacob Wilcox Ricketts should have ventured into a trade in which he had no experience at a time when, so far as Bristol was concerned, the markets were contracting. That he was successful cannot be denied, since when he retired he drew considerably more than he had invested, and certainly more than his partners were eventually to receive when the business closed down. He survived by eliminating his competitors, but this cannot disguise the fact that he made his money when the Bristol share of the total national market was declining. He was, it can be said, one of the last of a long line of successful merchant venturers, whose era was coming to an end because the circumstances that bred them, in so far as Bristol was concerned, were coming to an end. Jacob Wilcox Ricketts was a tobacco merchant, a banker, a brewer and a glassmaker. He fathered eight children and died, at the age of eighty-six, on 30th August, 1839, having, in the words of his grandson, buried thirty-nine partners. Politically he supported the Whigs, but sought no part in Bristol civic affairs. When he withdrew from the glass concern he was seventy-two years old, and it seems that he then began to sever all his business connections. He retired from the Castle Bank in 1826, when it was taken over by Stuckey's, and in August of the same year made over the whole of his interests in the brewery in equal shares to members of his family.[58]

The glass concern was reformed with the addition of two new partners, Henry Glascodine and John Gunning. Both had been with the concern for some years, the former apparently as secretary and accountant, and the latter as glassworks manager. This partnership ran unchanged until John Cave died in 1842 at the age of seventy-seven, and was succeeded by his son William. Because of ill health John Gunning withdrew at the end of the following year. He received £2, 600 as his share.[59] In 1845, Henry Ricketts' son Richard joined the partnership, and it is mostly from his notes that the final years of the company can be traced. Under an agreement drawn up in 1847 the glasshouses were to be managed by Richard Ricketts and Henry Glascodine, who were to 'devote the whole of the usual hours to the management and conduct of the business', for which they were to receive £400 a year, irrespective of profits. The same sum was to be paid to Henry Ricketts, who was to 'continue to manage and inspect the concern', although both Henry Ricketts and William Cave 'shall not be required to devote more of their time to the business than they or either of them shall think proper'. This agreement quotes the share capital as £24, 000, which can be compared with £34, 000 in 1834, and £64, 622 for the peak year, 1820.[60]

From 1841 to 1845 trading losses amounted to £5, 380. The next three years were profitable to the extent of £1, 964 but, from 1849 to 1851, losses of £3, 945 were incurred.[61] The Phoenix glasshouse was by now a shadow of its former self and Bristol, once the dominant glass making area in England, was now a backwater, with only three glasshouses in use. Even Henry Ricketts appears to have lost interest, since in 1833 he produced no evidence to put before the Commissioners of Inquiry into the Excise Establishment, despite his caustic comments some twelve years earlier. It was left to William Powell to give evidence, and he was a bottle maker with experience of flint glass only through his cutting shop, which had been closed for some years. Consistent heavy losses led to the closure of the flint glasshouse at Temple Gate in 1851. Richard Ricketts purchased the bottle stock, materials and utensils for £6, 465.18.0. and continued to run the Avon Street glasshouse under his own name.[62] Two years later he amalgamated with the neighbouring glasshouse, then run by William Powell, his son William, and Edward Filer. The new concern was known as Powells, Ricketts and Filer. William Powell senior died in 1854 and Edward Filer in 1856, after which the concern was renamed Powell and Ricketts. Commenting on the amalgamation, A. C. Powell wrote: 'For a long period there had been a fierce competition between the two firms, and much unfriendliness, to their mutual disadvantage. At last it was decided to unite their forces, and the event was celebrated by a feast, the relation of whose mighty proportions was a favourite subject with some of the old men'.[63]

Six years after the amalgamation Henry Ricketts died, at the age of seventy-six. If his father's aim had been to create a dynasty then in this he did not succeed. Given the circumstances the inheritance was bound to fail, nor was it helped by the long dispute. Henry, unlike his father, took an interest in civic affairs. He was member of the Bristol Corporation from 1832 to 1835 and an alderman at the time of his death. Not a great deal is known of these activities, although Latimer records an event in 1836 in which Henry Ricketts figured prominently. An equal number of Tories and Liberals had been elected to the Council and this created a deadlock in the election of Aldermen. After the election of one Liberal, Richard Ricketts, and one Tory, Henry Ricketts changed sides and voted with the Tories with the eventual result that Tory Aldermen outnumbered the Liberals by thirteen to three.[64] Following his death this notice appeared:

> 'A remarkable sale of wine took place . . . consequent upon the death of Alderman Henry Ricketts . . . The chief competition was for the port wine, which included samples of all the celebrated vintages between 1793 and 1836. Magnums of 1820 brought the unprecedented price of £3. 8. 0. each. One lot of the vintage of 1812 fetched £18. 10. 0 per dozen ordinary bottles. The entire stock of 180 dozen of port averaged £8 a dozen, the purchasers being chiefly Lancashire manufacturers'.[65]

Irony, perhaps, that Lancashire, having been one of the principal areas that wrested the glass trade from Bristol, should now take Henry Ricketts' wines as well. Was the quarrel with his father ever resolved? In 1833, when he left the centre of Bristol, it was to Brislington that he moved, which was as far to the east of Bristol as was Jacob Wilcox Ricketts' house on the west. Towards the end Henry Ricketts' health failed and in his correspondence with his daughter Ann, married to the Rector of Bishops Cleeve, there are frequent references to the pain in his back and limbs, and he is clearly very handicapped. Ann is obviously fond of her father and, in his own way, so too is her husband—but then he appears to have benefitted very well financially from the marriage. Whilst Ann's letters are much concerned with her father's ill health, the Rector of Bishops Cleeve recounts his shooting exploits, which appear to occur fairly frequently. There is no mention of pastoral care for his parishioners, but perhaps he judged which subjects his father-in-law found the more interesting.[66]

It is more difficult to get to grips with Richard Ricketts, who remains a man within the shadows. Any attempt to formulate his character is hampered, rather than assisted, by the querulous notes that he left amongst his father's papers. He seems to have less affection for his parent than does his sister. He complains, for example, that he was promised £125 a year on his marriage, but that this was never paid. However, the notes give some idea of the problems the glass concern experienced in its final years. He writes: 'When I joined the Concern July 1845 they had lost heavily for years—they never told me so—or would my Father allow me even to see the books with Mr Glascodine. Their bad debts where 3 or 4,000£ dreadfull' (*sic*). Either Henry Ricketts does not appear to have learnt anything from the dispute with his father, or the generation gap was a hereditary feature in the Ricketts family. Richard Ricketts continued with the bottle works until he died, some three years only after his father. The valedictory to this episode in the story of glassmaking in Bristol lies with him: 'Grandfather Ricketts left about £250,000 behind him but tis nearly all gone the Ricketts were too grand and lived in too fine places ever to be rich'.[67]

NOTES

Abbreviations:

BGAS	Bristol and Gloucestershire Archaeological Society.
BRO	Bristol Record Office.
BRS	Bristol Record Society.
FFBJ	*Felix Farley's Bristol Journal.*
JSGT	*Journal of the Society of Glass Technology.*
MBD	*Mathews' Bristol Directory.*
BM	*Bristol Mirror.*

1. The term *'flint glass'* had a particular meaning in regard to the Excise regulations, which were then in force. It covered clear, enamel, paste and stained glass for domestic use, and glass phials, small bottles used mostly for medicines and toilet waters.
2. H. J. Powell, *Glass making in England,* Cambridge (1923), p. 99.
3. H. Owen, *Two centuries of ceramic art in Bristol,* Gloucester, Bellows (1873), p. 386.
4. BRO: MS 12143. Commentary on the fortunes of the Phoenix glasshouse and those involved with it is mostly drawn from this source. Subsidiary references are given where appropriate. My grateful thanks go to the City Archivist, Miss Mary E. Williams, and her staff, for the facility for studying these papers on numerous occasions. I should like to thank also the Librarian and staff of the Avon County Reference Library, Bristol.
5. H. Owen: *op. cit.*
6. FFBJ: 2nd December, 1758.
7. FFBJ: 11th January, 1783.
8. BRO: MS 12143 (I).
9. *Ibid.* (6).
10. *Ibid.* (7) (8) (9).
11. *Crown glass* was used for glazing windows.
12. BGAS: *Transactions,* 29 (1906), p. 130.
13. B. W. E. Alford, 'The flint and bottle glass industry in the early nineteenth century: a case study of a Bristol firm', *Business History,* 10 (1968), p. 13.
14. C. H. Cave, *A history of banking in Bristol,* Bristol (1899).
15. A. B. Beavan, *Bristol lists,* Bristol (1899). Most references to civic careers have been taken from this source.
16. Statistical data relating to the glass industry have been taken from: *Thirteenth report of the Commissioners of Inquiry into the excise establishment* (1835); B. R. Mitchell & P. Deane, *Abstract of British historical statistics,* Cambridge, University Press (1962), p. 267; G. R. Porter, *The progress of the nation,* London, John Murray (1847).
17. FFBJ: 7th January, 1786.

18. FFBJ: 19th September, 1789.
19. FFBJ: 19th September, 1789.
20. For a more detailed discussion of these events, see C. Weeden, 'The problems of consolidation in the Bristol flint glass industry', *Glass Technology*, 22 (1981), pp. 236-8.
21. BRO: MS 12143 (9) (10).
22. P. Davis, *The development of the American glass industry*, Cambridge, Mass., Harvard University Press (1949), p. 56.
23. BRO: MS 12143 (8) (9) (10) (11).
24. A. C. Powell, 'Glassmaking in Bristol', *BGAS Transactions*, 47 (1926), p. 219.
25. BRO: MS 12143 (41).
26. I. V. Hall, 'The Daubeny's', *BGAS Transactions*, 84 (1965), pp. 113-140; 85 (1966), pp. 175-201.
27. C. H. Cave, *op. cit.*,
28. BRO: MS 12143 (43).
29. FFBJ: 13th February, 1802.
30. BRO: MS 12143 (13).
31. *Ibid.* (7) (8) (9) (10) (11) (12).
32. *Ibid.* (41).
33. *Ibid.* (40) £18, 794 quoted in company accounts (1815/16; 1816/17); £16, 631 receipt on final discharge dated 17th February, 1818.
34. *Ibid.* (40), detailed accounts of company, 1813 to 1824.
35. MBD: 1820: Benjamin Bickley, Merchant, Princes Street, Bristol; Stephens and Goodhind, Attornies, 19 Small Street, Bristol.
36. BRO: MS 12143 (43) This section includes the correspondence relating to the dispute between Jacob Wilcox Ricketts and his son Henry Ricketts.
37. MBD: 1820: Joseph S. Usher, Attorney, 17 Clare Street, Bristol.
38. BRO: MS 12143 (41).
39. *Ibid.* (43) 5 August, 1802.
40. *Ibid.* (41).
41. A. C. Powell, *op. cit.*, p. 236.
42. BSO: MS 12143 (43), 18th November, 1821.
43. *Ibid.* (43), undated but probably between 7th and 9th October, 1821.
44. *Ibid.* (40).
45. HM Patent No. 4623, granted 5th December, 1821.
46. Olive Jones has kindly drawn my attention to a similar mechanism credited to Charles Chubsee of Stourbridge and dated 1802; see G. Weiss (tr. J. Seligman), *The book of glass*, London, Barrie and Jenkins (1971), p. 323.
47. BRO: MS 12143 (43), 6th November, 1821. Possibly the Chubsee mould was used at the Phoenix glasshouse for making the small flint bottles. Henry Ricketts' patent specifically refers to the larger, or common bottle as it was termed, made at the Avon Street glasshouse. It is conceivable that the 'trifling improvement' to which John Cave refers was the adaptation of the Chubsee mould for larger bottles.
48. BRO: MS 12143 (40).
49. B. W. E. Alford, *op. cit.*, p. 16.
50. BRO: MS 12143 (13), 1st May, 1811.
51. 43 George III c. 122. Profits were taxed at the rate of one shilling in the pound, increased in 1806 to two shillings.
52. FFBJ: 5th June, 1802.
53. BRO: MS 12143 (40).
54. *Ibid.* (40).
55. *Ibid.* (43).
56. *Ibid.* (17) (40).
57. For detailed examination of the relative decline of Bristol as a trading centre see:— B. W. E. Alford, 'The economic development of Bristol in the nineteenth century—an enigma', in *Essays in Bristol and Gloucestershire History* (ed. P. McGrath and J. Cannon), BGAS (1976); P. T. Marcy, 'Bristol's roads and communications on the eve of the industrial revolution 1740-70', *BGAS Transactions*, 87 (1968); W. E. Minchinton, 'Politics and the port of Bristol in the eighteenth century', BRS, 23 (1963); W. E. Minchinton, 'The trade of Bristol in the eighteenth century', BRS, 20 (1957); A. F. Williams, 'Bristol port plans and improvement schemes of the eighteenth century', *BGAS Transactions*, 81 (1962).
58. BRO: MS 12143 (41).
59. *Ibid.* (20), 12th December, 1843.
60. *Ibid.* (22), 25th October, 1847.
61. *Ibid.* (41).
62. *Ibid.* (40); BM: 12th June, 1852:—

    'Phoenix Flint Glass Works, Temple-gate, Bristol. Sale of Glass Ware
    In consequence of the dissolution of the Partnership Concern of the Flint Glass Works carried on for many years by Henry Ricketts and Co., the remaining portion of their manufactured stock is now for sale at considerably reduced prices, consisting of cut decanters, dinner carofts, water jugs, dessert dishes, butters and sugars, milk and cream jugs, pickle bottles, cruets and castors, salts, finger basins, tumblers, goblets, wine, champagne, claret, jelly, custard and other glasses, smelling and toilet bottles, plain, frosted and cut hanging and other lamps, hemispheres, shades, lamp chimnies etc. etc. and a variety of other articles of plain and cut glass of the first quality. Also suited [for] the Druggists—vials, carboys, stoppered bottles, fancy moulded bottles for drugs, oils, perfumes etc.
    The stock of plain articles for cutting consists of decanters, water ewers, milk and cream jugs, water carofts, wine, claret and champagne glasses and other articles.
    The Phoenix Glass Bottle Works, formerly carried on by the above Firm, are continued in all their branches by Richard Ricketts and Co., St Philip's, Bristol.

    I am indebted to Philip Whatmoor for calling my attention to this notice.
63. A. C. Powell, *op. cit.*, p. 245.
64. J. Latimer, *Annals of Bristol in the nineteenth century*, Bristol (1887), p. 211.
65. J. Latimer, *op. cit.*, p. 369.
66. BRO: MS 12143 (48).
67. *Ibid.* (41).

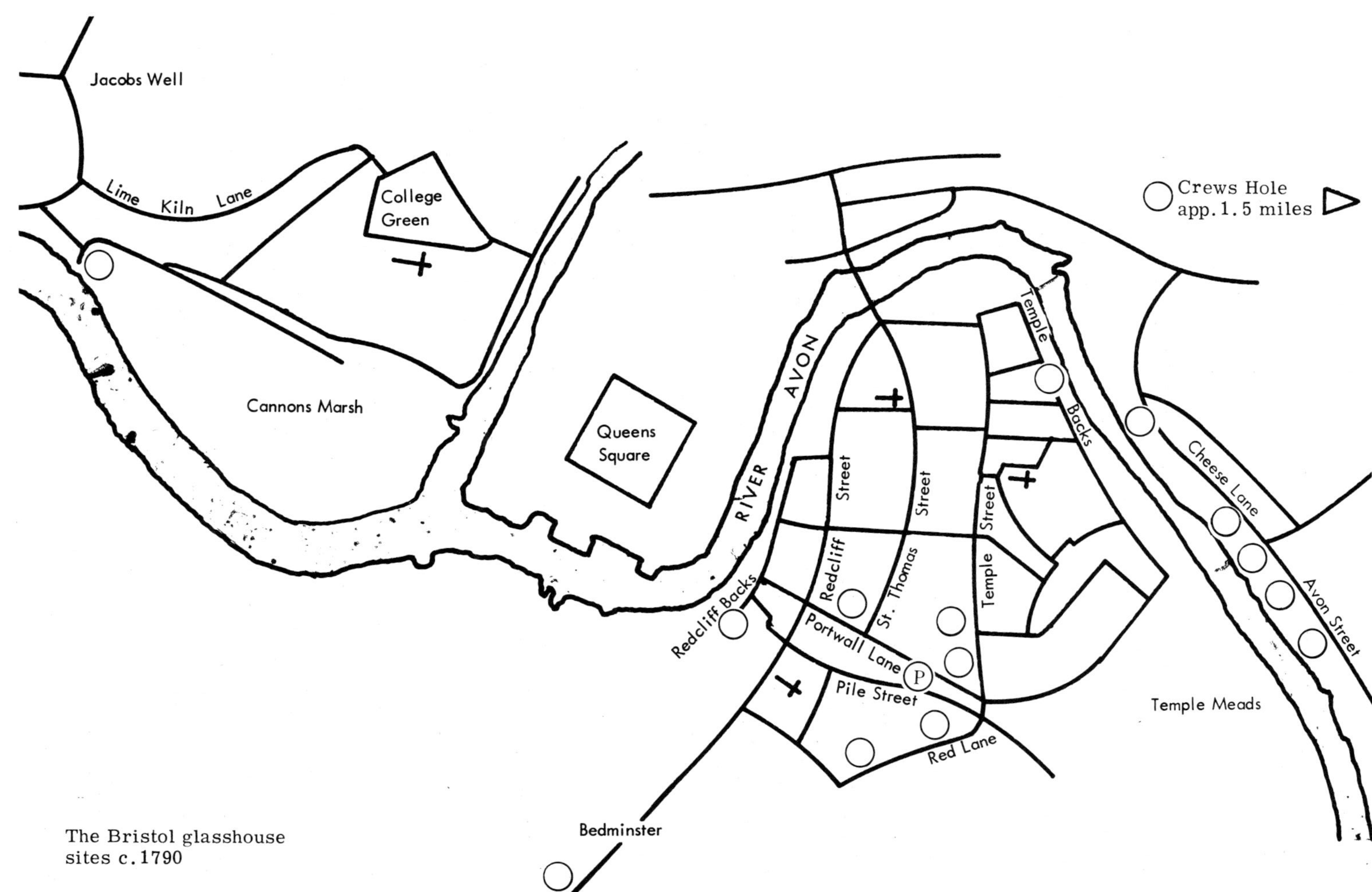

Figure 1. Map of Bristol showing glasshouses about 1790. The Phoenix Glasshouse is marked "P".

Figure 2. Goblet engraved with a view of the Phoenix Glasshouse. Bristol City Museum and Art Gallery.

Figure 3. Token of the Phoenix Glasshouse, about 1800. Courtesy of Lady Elton.

Figure 4. Portrait of Jacob Wilcox Ricketts (after illustration in C. H. Cave, *A History of Banking in Bristol*, 1899, the painting then said to be in the possession of Mrs. L. H. Ricketts).

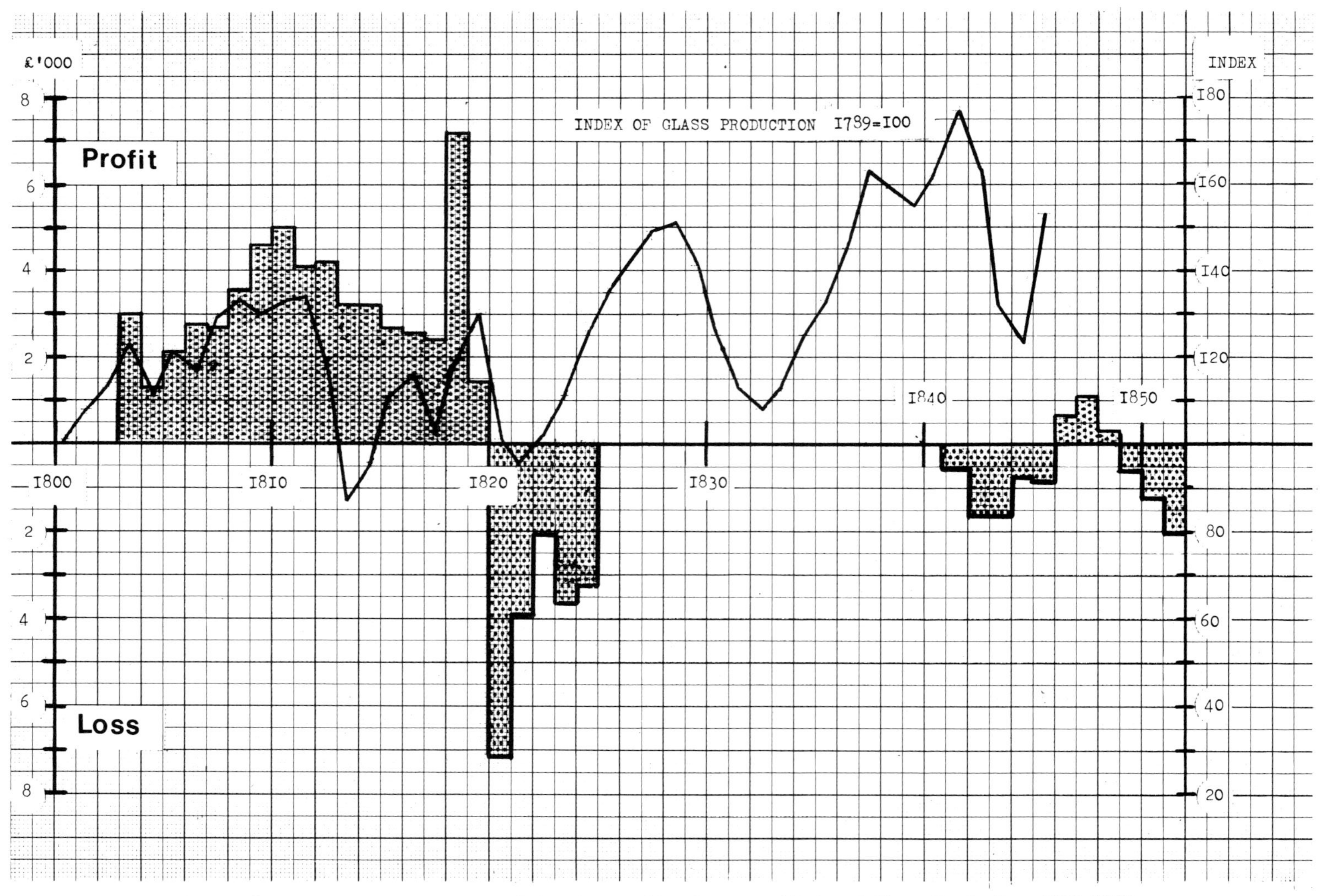

Figure 5. Profit and loss accounts of the Phoenix Glasshouse, and Index of Glass Production, 1789-1845.

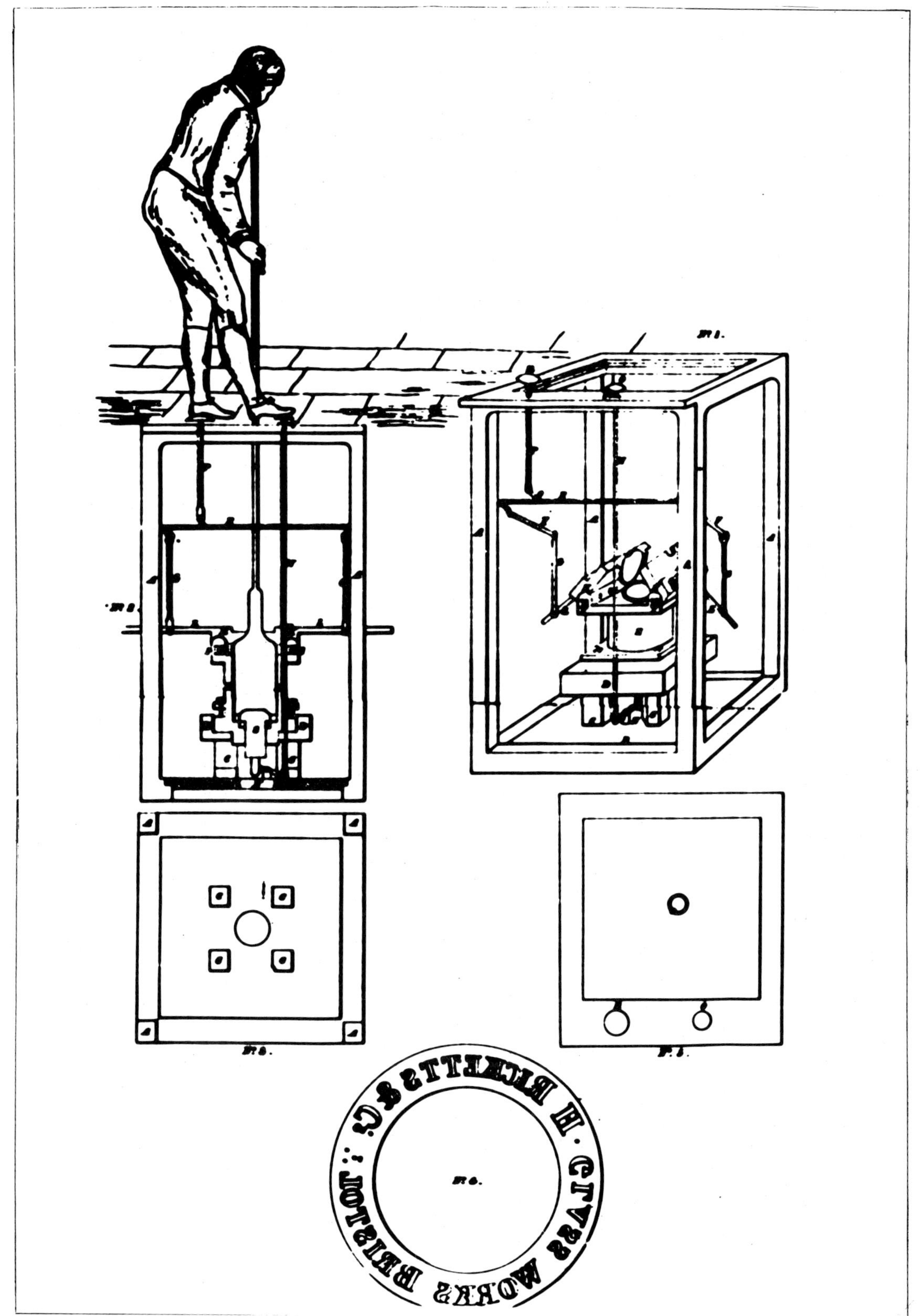

Figure 6. Henry Ricketts' Patent Specification, 1821.

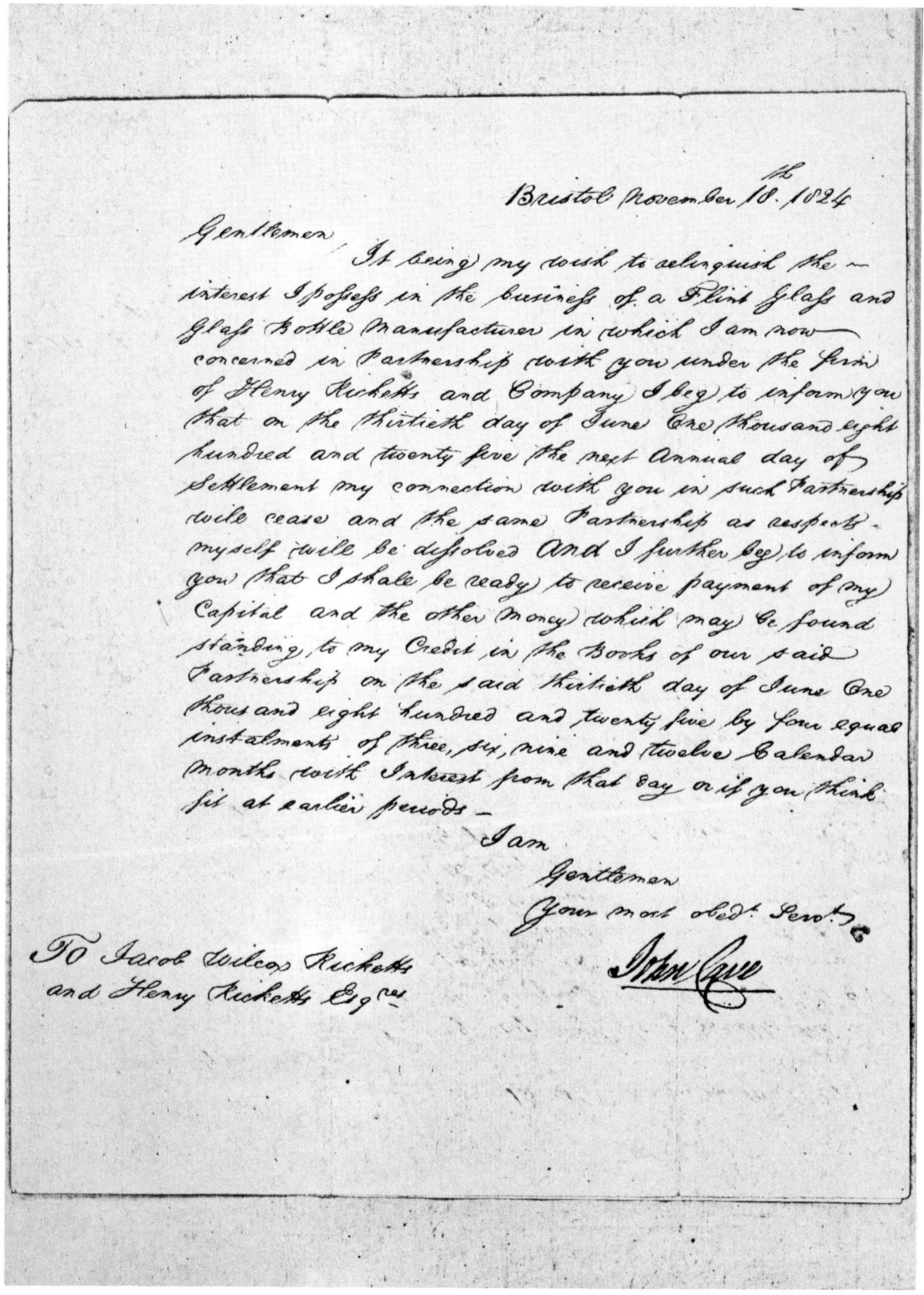

Bristol November 18th 1824

Gentlemen

It being my wish to relinquish the interest I possess in the business of a Flint Glass and Glass Bottle Manufacturer in which I am now concerned in Partnership with you under the firm of Henry Ricketts and Company I beg to inform you that on the thirtieth day of June One thousand eight hundred and twenty five the next Annual day of Settlement my connection with you in such Partnership will cease and the same Partnership as respects myself will be dissolved And I further beg to inform you that I shall be ready to receive payment of my Capital and the other money which may be found standing to my Credit in the Books of our said Partnership on the said thirtieth day of June One thousand eight hundred and twenty five by four equal instalments of three, six, nine and twelve Calendar Months with Interest from that day or if you think fit at earlier periods —

I am

Gentlemen

Your most obedt. Servt.

John Cave

To Jacob Wilcox Ricketts
and Henry Ricketts Esqres

Figure 7. John Cave's letter of resignation, dated 18 November, 1824. Bristol Record Office MS12143(43)

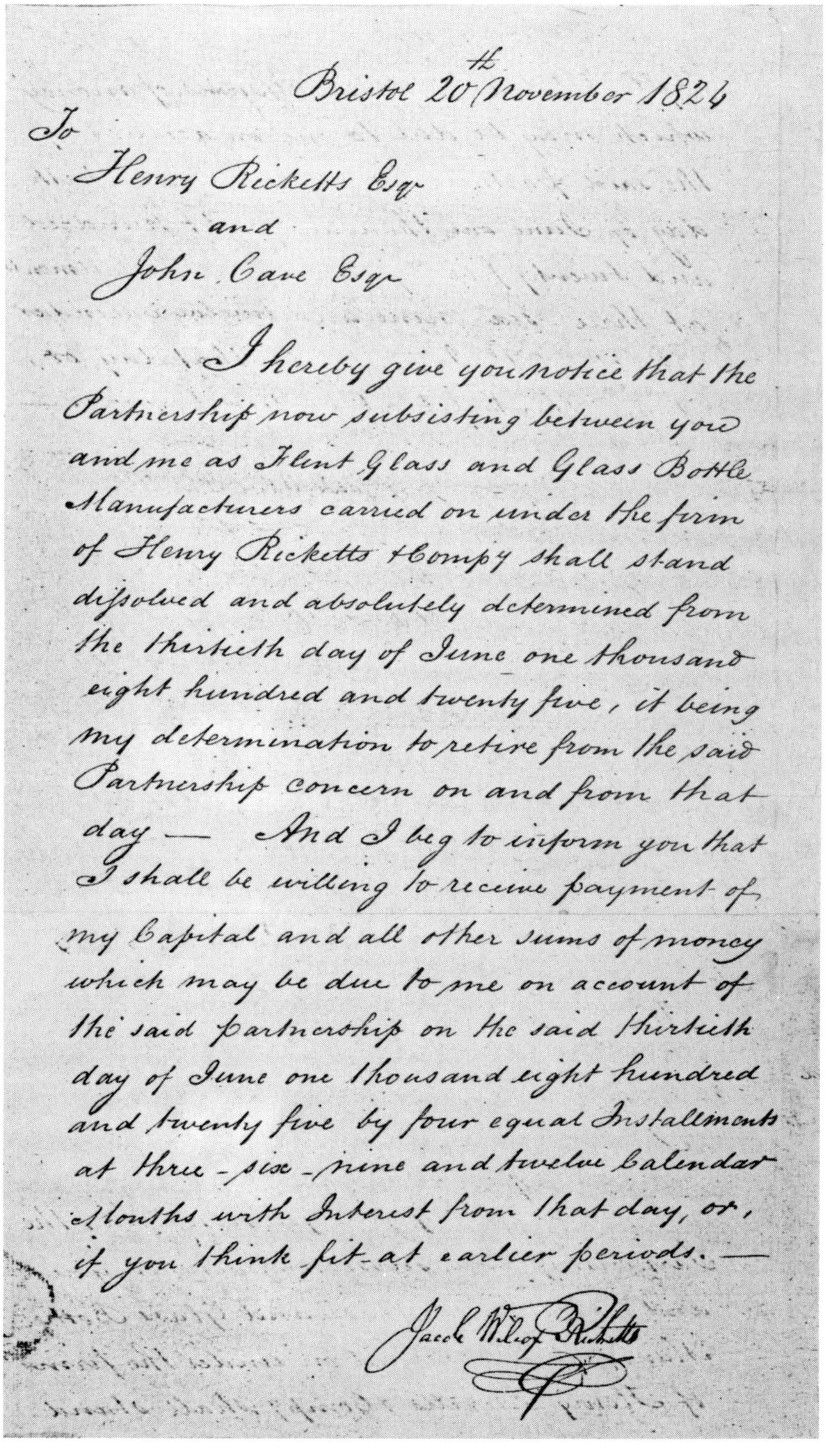

Bristol 20th November 1824

To

Henry Ricketts Esqr

and

John Cave Esqr

I hereby give you notice that the Partnership now subsisting between you and me as Flint Glass and Glass Bottle Manufacturers carried on under the firm of Henry Ricketts & Compy shall stand dissolved and absolutely determined from the thirtieth day of June one thousand eight hundred and twenty five, it being my determination to retire from the said Partnership concern on and from that day — And I beg to inform you that I shall be willing to receive payment of my Capital and all other sums of money which may be due to me on account of the said partnership on the said thirtieth day of June one thousand eight hundred and twenty five by four equal Installments at three - six - nine and twelve Calendar Months with Interest from that day, or, if you think fit at earlier periods. —

Jacob Wilcox Ricketts

Figure 8. Jacob Wilcox Ricketts' letter of resignation, dated 20 November, 1824. Bristol Record Office MS12143(43)

A. Henning

Ornamental goldfish bowl, engraved
with naturalistic pond life.
Unknown engraver. English late 19th century.

48 Walton Street, Walton-on-the Hill, Tadworth, Surrey
Phone Tadworth 3337 (STD 073 781)

Sheppard and Cooper Ltd
5-6 Cork Street
London W1
Tel: 01-734 9179

An English facet stem wine glass, stipple engraved with a horse in a landscape by David Wolff c. 1785.
A glass with similar engraving is in the Rijksmuseum, Amsterdam, and has an inscription on the back which includes the name "D. Wolf".

DELOMOSNE AND SON LTD

FINE ANTIQUES

EUROPEAN CHINA AND GLASS
NEEDLEWORK PICTURES
CHANDELIERS

Members of
The British Antique Dealers' Association

Three fine goblets decorated in imitation of engraving by a method the patent for which was taken out by John Davenport *c.*1806. The sporting subjects are wildfowling, fishing and coursing and the reverse sides depict rustic cottages. The bizarre formal borders are typical of this factory. Height $6\frac{1}{8}$ ins.

4 CAMPDEN HILL ROAD, KENSINGTON HIGH STREET,
LONDON W8 7DU 01-937 1804 CABLES: DELOMOSNE LONDON W8

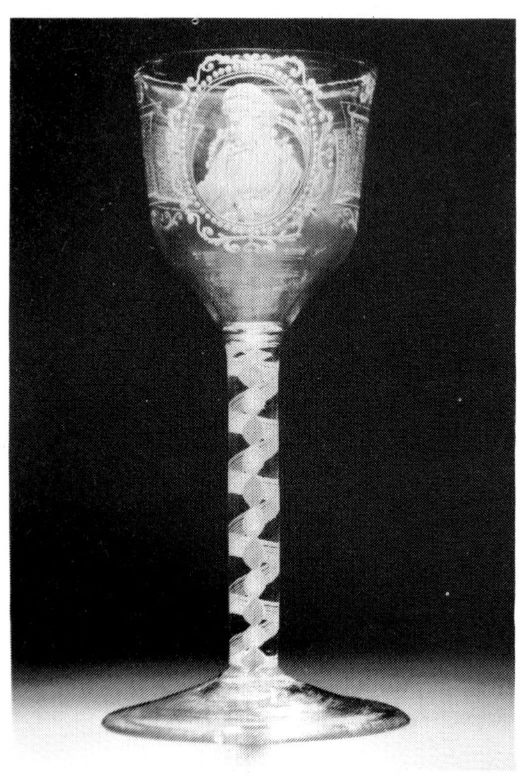

MAUREEN THOMPSON

has now moved from 34 Kensington Church Street, London W.8.

to

SUN HOUSE
HALL STREET
LONG MELFORD
SUFFOLK

Tel. Sudbury (0787) 78252

Where she will continue to specialise in
18th and 19th Century Glass

Heavy baluster goblet. The funnel bowl solid at the base mounted on a squat inverted baluster containing an air tear. Folded foot.

*c.*1700

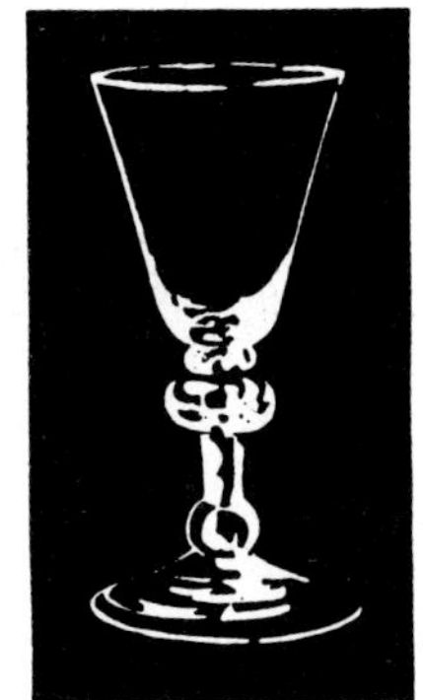

John A Brooks

ANTIQUE GLASS

2, KNIGHTS CRESCENT, ROTHLEY, LEICESTERSHIRE.

Telephone: Leicester (0533) 302625. By appointment only.

Although the emphasis of my stock is on 18th Century glass, I also deal in a wide variety of 19th Century glass. including later decorative and pressed glass. I always have a wide range of items priced to appeal to the modest investor as well as the discerning specialist collector. I also deal in second-hand and out-of-print books on glass.

I exhibit at major antiques fairs throughout the country but I am pleased to see callers at the above address by appointment.

Details of stocks and fairs will be sent on request.

Jeanette Hayhurst

Fine Glass

The Knightsbridge Pavilion

112, Brompton Rd., S. W. 3.

01 584 1156

18th century Drinking Glasses,

18th & 19th century Decanters & Table Glass.

Catalogues & book lists on request.

Asprey

BY APPOINTMENT
TO H.M. THE QUEEN
GOLDSMITHS, SILVERSMITHS
& JEWELLERS
ASPREY & COMPANY LIMITED
LONDON

BY APPOINTMENT
TO H.M. QUEEN ELIZABETH
THE QUEEN MOTHER
JEWELLERS
ASPREY & COMPANY LIMITED
LONDON

BY APPOINTMENT
TO H.R.H. THE PRINCE OF WALES
JEWELLERS, GOLDSMITHS
& SILVERSMITHS
ASPREY & COMPANY LIMITED
LONDON

A fine acorn baluster wine glass, English circa 1710.
Height: $6\frac{3}{4}$ ins.

ASPREY & COMPANY P.L.C.,
London W1Y 0AR
Telegrams: 25110 Asprey G.

165-169 New Bond Street,
Tel: 01-493 6767
Telex: 25110 Asprey G.

To the Efteemed READERS of the GLASS CIRCLE [4]

The Editors of this Review refpectfully take this Public method of informing the Nobility, Gentry and all Purchafers of the Work that there remain a few copies of the Glass Circle [1], [2] and [3]

Containing among other curious Articles by Eminent Authorities—

The Glass Circle 1

THE HOARE BILLS FOR GLASS
by the late W. A. Thorpe

ENAMELLING AND GILDING ON GLASS
by R. J. Charlefton

GLASS AND BRITISH PHARMACY 1600-1900
by J. K. Crellin and J. R. Scott

ENGLISH ALE GLASSES 1685-1830
by P. C. Trubridge

SCENT BOTTLES
by Edmund Launert

The Glass Circle 2

A GLASSMAKER'S BANKRUPTCY SALE
by R. J. Charleston

THE BATHGATE BOWL
by Barbara Morris

THE ENGLISH ALE GLASSES, GROUP 3
The Tall Balusters and Flute-Glasses for Champagne and Ale
by P. C. Trubridge

THE PUGH GLASSHOUSES IN DUBLIN
by Mary Boydell

GLASS IN 18TH CENTURY NORWICH
by Sheenah Smith

WHO WAS GEORGE RAVENSCROFT?
by Rosemary Rendel

HOW DID GEORGE RAVENSCROFT DISCOVER LEAD CRYSTAL?
by D. C. Watts

The Glass Circle 3

THE APSLEY PELLATTS
by J. A. H. Rose

DECORATION OF GLASS, PART 4: PRINTING ON GLASS
by R. J. Charleston

DECORATION OF GLASS, PART 5: ACID-ETCHING
by R. J. Charleston

THE JACOBITE ENGRAVERS
by G. B. Seddon

"MEN OF GLASS": A PERSONAL VIEW OF THE DE BONGAR FAMILY IN THE 16TH AND 17TH CENTURIES
by G. Bungard

THE ENGLISH ALE GLASSES, GROUP 4. ALE/BEER GLASSES IN THE 19TH CENTURY
by P. C. Trubridge

Available from Messrs. Unwin Brothers, The Gresham Press, Old Woking, Surrey, GU22 9LH

For *The Glass Circle* 1 price £4 (£2.50 to Members of the Glass Circle).
For *The Glass Circle* 2 price £4.50 (£3 to Members of the Glass Circle).
For *The Glass Circle* 3 price £6 (£4.50 to Members of the Glass Circle) plus current postage for 400, 450, and 500 grams weight respectively.